MW01257914

Ether: *a brief theological introduction*

This publication was made possible by generous support from the Laura F. Willes Center for Book of Mormon Studies, part of the Neal A. Maxwell Institute for Religious Scholarship at Brigham Young University.

Published by the Neal A. Maxwell Institute for Religious Scholarship, Brigham Young University, Provo, Utah. The copyright for the 2013 text of The Book of Mormon is held by The Church of Jesus Christ of Latter-day Saints, Salt Lake City, Utah; that text is quoted throughout and used by permission.

The Maxwell Institute's *The Book of Mormon: brief theological introductions* series offered by Brigham Young University is not made, provided, approved, or endorsed by Intellectual Reserve Inc. or The Church of Jesus Christ of Latter-day Saints. Any content or opinions expressed, implied, or included in or with this book are solely those of the author and are not necessarily those of Brigham Young University or any of its affiliates, Intellectual Reserve, Inc., or The Church of Jesus Christ of Latter-day Saints.

Printed in the United States of America

ISBN: 978-0-8425-0017-3

LIBRARY OF CONGRESS CONTROL NUMBER: 2020902735

Ether

a brief theological introduction

BRIGHAM YOUNG UNIVERSITY

NEAL A. MAXWELL INSTITUTE

PROVO, UTAH

Rosalynde Frandsen Welch

The Book of Mormon: brief theological introductions series seeks Christ in scripture by combining intellectual rigor and the disciple's yearning for holiness. It answers Elder Neal A. Maxwell's call to explore the book's "divine architecture": "There is so much more in the Book of Mormon than we have yet discovered. The book's divine architecture and rich furnishings will increasingly unfold to our view, further qualifying it as *'a marvelous work and a wonder.'* (Isaiah 29:14) . . . All the rooms in this mansion need to be explored, whether by valued traditional scholars or by those at the cutting edge. Each plays a role, and one LDS scholar cannot say to the other, *'I have no need of thee.'"* 1 (1 Corinthians 12:21)

For some time, faithful scholars have explored the book's textual history, reception, historicity, literary quality, and more. This series focuses particularly on theology—the scholarly practice of exploring a scriptural text's implications and its lens on God's work in the world. Series volumes invite Latter-day Saints to discover additional dimensions of this treasured text but leave to prophets and apostles their unique role of declaring its definitive official doctrines. In this case, theology, as opposed to authoritative doctrine, relates to the original sense of the term as, literally, reasoned "God talk." The word also designates a well-developed academic field, but it is the more general sense of the term that most often applies here. By engaging each scriptural book's theology on its own terms, this series explores the spiritual and intellectual force of the ideas appearing in the Latter-day Saints' "keystone" scripture.

Series authors and editors possess specialized professional training that informs their work but, significantly, each takes Christ as theology's proper end because he is the proper end of all scripture and all reflection on it. We, too, "talk of Christ, we rejoice in Christ, we preach of Christ...that our children may know to what source they may look for a remission of their sins" (2 Nephi 25:26). Moreover, while experts in the modern disciplines of philosophy, theology, literature, and history, series authors and editors also work explicitly within the context of personal and institutional commitments both to Christian discipleship and to The Church of Jesus Christ of Latter-day Saints. These volumes are not official Church publications but can be best understood in light of these deep commitments. And because we acknowledge that scripture demands far more than intellectual experimentation, we call readers' attention to the processes of conversion and sanctification at play on virtually every scriptural page.

Individual series authors offer unique approaches but, taken together, they model a joint invitation to readers to engage scripture in their own way. No single approach to theology or scriptural interpretation commands preeminence in these volumes. No volume pretends to be the final word on theological reflection for its part of the Book of Mormon. Varied perspectives and methodologies are evident throughout. This is intentional. In addition, though we recognize love for the Book of Mormon is a "given" for most Latter-day Saint readers, we also share the conviction that, like the gospel of Jesus Christ itself, the Book of Mormon is inexhaustible.[2] These volumes invite readers to slow down and read scripture more thoughtfully and transformatively. Elder Maxwell cautioned against reading the Book of Mormon as "hurried tourists" who scarcely venture beyond "the entry hall."[3] To that end, we dedicate this series to his apostolic conviction that there is always more to learn from the Book of Mormon and much to be gained from our faithful search for Christ in its pages.

—The Editors

Contents

Introduction

The book of Ether goes over like a lead balloon. It's freighted with the history of two millennia, mired with lurid violence. The story is heavy—ill-suited, perhaps, to show the "great things" of God's deliverance, as the title page of the Book of Mormon promises. Surely it is too earthbound for greatness.

The book lifts off, nonetheless. Passages of spiritual reflection concentrated near its beginning and end open fresh views on Christ and the salvation he offers. In the opening story of the brother of Jared, sixteen stones are miraculously illuminated to reveal a vision of Jesus Christ himself. In the book's twelfth chapter, examples of mighty faith prompt us to reconsider strength and weakness in light of Christ's grace. In the thirteenth chapter, prophetic vision promises the ultimate reconciliation of old and new in holy cities chartered by God's covenant. Throughout, the book's self-aware narrator explores the workings of scripture itself.

the book of Ether: first considerations
The book of Ether is the Book of Mormon's miniature, a book-within-a-book recorded on plates-within-the-plates. It recounts the history of an ancient people that both echoes and prefigures the broad contours of Nephite migration, society, and demise. It holds a mirror to the Book of Mormon's own origin and reception. And it has fascinated readers from the moment of its discovery. The Nephites initially become aware of an

extinct indigenous society when an engraved stone is discovered in Zarahemla and presented to Mosiah$_1$. ☞ He interprets the engravings, which recount the lineage of one Coriantumr, the last king and sole survivor of an ancient people (see Omni 1:21–22). The Mulekite people, we are told, encounter Coriantumr himself and harbor the wandering king for a time.

Later, additional artifacts are discovered by separatist Nephites in a ruined city littered with bones. Among the artifacts are twenty-four gold plates engraved with indecipherable characters. They are delivered to King Mosiah$_2$, who translates the plates with the aid of divine instruments called "interpreters" (Mosiah 8:7–18). The plates contain a fuller history of the ancient people. Mosiah$_2$'s translation does not circulate widely, despite the evident mystique the lost inhabitants hold for the Nephites. Much later, Moroni will learn in the course of his editorial work that the brother of Jared's mighty vision, recorded in the Jaredite record, was forbidden from public knowledge until Christ should make it manifest at his ministry to the Nephites (Ether 4:1).[1] For this reason, perhaps, the content of the record remains mostly unfamiliar to Nephites. Notably, the brother of Jared's encounter with Jesus Christ, the spiritual apex of the book of Ether, seems to have remained entirely unknown to—or at least unremarked upon by—earlier Nephite prophets, who focus instead on the destructive secret combinations contained in the Jaredite plates (see Alma 37:21). As the Jaredite plates are transmitted with the larger trove of records through the centuries, the story of the lost people lingers in Nephite scribal culture with an air of archaic mystique.

☞ In order to distinguish between persons with the same name in the Book of Mormon, I use subscript numerals to indicate which chronological bearer of the name I refer to. Here, Mosiah$_1$ is the father of king Benjamin and grandfather of the king Mosiah$_2$ who figures prominently in the book of Mosiah. Similarly, Lehi$_1$ (of Jerusalem) is differentiated from Lehi$_4$ (son of Helaman);

It falls to Moroni, son of Mormon and last of the Nephite prophet-scribes, to bring the ancient record to light. He writes to fulfill his father's promise earlier in the Book of Mormon that the Jaredite account "shall be written hereafter; for behold, it is expedient that all people should know the things which are written in this account" (Mosiah 28:19). Moroni writes with a singular focus. After inheriting responsibility for the plates and the editorial production of the Book of Mormon, he wraps up the book named for his father with a decisive shift. While Mormon grieves the past destruction of the Nephite people and looks ahead to the recovery of the remnant of Lehi$_1$, Moroni states brusquely, "Behold, I make an end of speaking concerning this people" (Morm. 8:13). Instead, he directs his prophetic attention to modern readers and the cultural circumstances of the future coming forth of the Book of Mormon (see Morm. 8–9). When Moroni turns to the ancient book of Ether, this latter-day context is still foremost in his mind. Functioning as both a highlight reel and an historical preview tucked just before the larger volume's end, the book of Ether takes the reader "back to the future" on a final wild ride recapping the lessons of Jaredite (and Nephite) history.

Moroni says little about the methods and circumstances of his editorial work on the book of Ether. He does not clarify whether he consults the prior translation of Mosiah$_2$, whether he makes use of Mosiah's interpreter instruments, or whether the twenty-four plates contain a single record or several distinct writings. He reports that his account is constrained by the dwindling space for inscription on the plates and the scarcity of ore to produce more (Morm. 8:5); moreover, he seems to suggest that he relies on his memory for some part of his work (Ether 5:1). His primary source is a record called the Book of Ether, compiled by the Jaredite

4

prophet of that name who witnessed the violent end of his civilization and survived to record its destruction. Ether's voice is largely absent from Moroni's rendition, however, which preserves only a single verse of first-person language from Ether and very little of his prophetic teaching (Ether 15:34; see Ether 12–13). Moroni concedes that "the hundredth part [of Ether's record] I have not written" (Ether 15:33).

It is Moroni's prophetic mind, then, that prevails in the book of Ether. As Mormon does with the large plates of Nephi, Moroni introduces interpretive comments to highlight lessons of Jaredite history. Unlike Mormon, however, Moroni directly addresses these comments to a particular readership and expands them at length in his own voice. Jaredite history is a grim march of intrigue and depravity, and Moroni's six inserted comments lend rhythm to the chronicle. The structure of the book of Ether may be summarized in the following way, with Moroni's comments in red:[2]

1:1–6	Moroni introduces the record of Ether; he omits material from creation to the great tower.
1:6–33	Genealogy of Ether's descent from Jared.
1:34–2:8	Jaredite departure from the great tower.
2:9–12	Moroni addresses the Gentiles: Jesus Christ is the God of the land.
2:13–3:16	Jared's brother prepares the barges and is visited by the premortal Jesus Christ.
3:17–20	Moroni compares the brother of Jared's vision to Christ's Nephite ministry.

Moroni and the Gentiles

Moroni's comments overwhelmingly address a specific readership, the modern readers of the Book of Mormon whom he calls "Gentiles": "And this cometh unto you, O ye Gentiles, that ye may know the decrees of God" (Ether 2:11). Moroni draws here on Nephite prophecies of God's deliverance of Israel in the last days. As recorded in the prophecies of Lehi₁, Nephi₁, and Jacob, and later reiterated by Jesus Christ himself, the Abrahamic covenant will be honored and extended to the entire human family through the collaboration of peoples outside the covenant known as the Gentiles (see 2 Ne. 30:2). Moroni, more than any other Book of Mormon author, turns his attention to the promises and warnings issued to this group.

Moroni's worldview foregrounds a set of ethnic categories in the land of promise, which he understands as a particular geographical place set apart by God. His ethical teachings and his prophecies of events in the modern world are rooted in the relationship between the Gentiles, who are relative newcomers to the land of promise, and the remnant of Lehi₁, who are the indigenous people of that land. The intertwined responsibilities, gifts, and spiritual destinies of the two groups are at the heart of his vision of salvation in Christ. To grasp the meaning of the book of Ether, then, readers must attend to its treatment of indigenous power and promise in two different historical contexts. First, the ancient Book of Ether 🔖 represents for Moroni the sacred history of an aboriginal society, the Jaredites, native to his people's homeland. Second, Moroni's comments to modern Gentiles portray the remnant of Lehi$_1$ as the "new" indigenous peoples who will lead the promised land to its sacred destiny. Ether 13 contains an extraordinary prophecy of the remnant of Joseph—now the indigenous inhabitants of the land that the Gentiles occupy—in which the despised and scattered seed of Lehi$_1$ will become the favored ushers of the second coming of Christ and the fulfillment of the Abrahamic covenant.

A caveat is in order, however. A theological interpreter must be thoughtful in her "likening" of the book of Ether to present-day society. Moroni's worldview does not map transparently onto modern understandings of ethnic identity and geography. The category of indigeneity is historically contingent: the Jaredites are indigenous relative to the Lehites, while centuries later the Lehites are indigenous relative to the Gentiles. Furthermore, Moroni's vision of the coming forth of the Book of Mormon is focused on the time and place of the early restoration. Today, however, the Book of Mormon is read around the world, in places and cultures far removed from the particular ethnic dynamics Moroni foresees.

🔖 To indicate the ancient record written by Ether. I'll refer to the "Book of Ether" (with the capitalized "Book"), in accordance with its capitalization in the text of the title page of the Book of Mormon. To indicate Moroni's redaction of that underlying record, I'll refer to the "book of Ether."

For the purposes of this theological study, then, I set aside specific matters of geography or population genetics in my use of the terms *Israel*, *seed of Lehi*, *Gentile*, and other ethnic categories. These terms appear frequently in the chapters that follow because they are central to the concerns of the book of Ether. In each context, I try to discern Moroni's understanding of the terms, without implying endorsement for any modern determination of their meaning. The text speaks with great moral vigor even when these interpretive categories remain open. Building on Nephite tradition, Moroni considers Israelites to be "insiders," those originally included in God's covenants with Abraham and Moses, while Gentiles are "outsiders," those who are drawn into God's saving plan through other means and missions. Moroni comes to understand that these boundaries are porous and that insiders of any group may, in another time or place, find themselves on the outside. His message for both groups is clear and insistent: God will never cease working to bring outsiders into his blessed presence. God instructs his insiders to act on his behalf to accomplish this end. All readers, in any context, may carry this message into the particular systems of power and exclusion that they inhabit.

Moroni the man

The book of Ether reflects the character and experience of its editor and narrator, Moroni. Despite the voluble self-expression of his inserted comments, Moroni writes little about the events of his life. Mormon reports that Moroni leads a legion of Nephites in the final battles with the Lamanites, and together they witness the destruction of their community (Morm. 6:11–12). Following the death of his father, Moroni wanders alone for decades through lands wrecked by violence and bloodshed (Morm. 8:5–8). He understands that his life has been spared so that he may "write the sad tale of the destruction of my people," and the preservation and completion of the Book of Mormon fills the remainder of his life (Morm. 8:3). He sees the spiritual decline of his people and the narrowing of his historical horizon in the literal depletion of the remaining plates that he fills one by one. The tragic saga of the once-blessed Nephites fades to black with the exhaustion of metallic ore. Though his experiences closely parallel those of the prophet Ether, Moroni shows little interest in biography and remains silent on his authorial resemblance to the last Jaredite prophet-scribe. Instead, Moroni identifies with the latter-day translator and custodian of the plates, Joseph Smith, whose experience he first considers in Mormon 8:16–26, and whom he admonishes directly in Ether 5.

In Moroni's remarks to readers, his character readily shows itself. Moroni is a time traveler, a ghost walking the border between two worlds: "I speak unto you as though I spake from the dead," he writes to his modern readers (Morm. 9:30). Having witnessed the apocalyptic destruction of his world, he is preoccupied with the apocalyptic future into which the Book of Mormon will emerge. His split-screen perspective straddles the distant past of the Jaredites and the distant future of the Gentiles. At times, his immersion in the nineteenth-century context of the early restoration is so complete that we might plausibly consider Moroni the first latter-day prophet: "Behold, I speak unto you as if ye were present," he writes to his latter-day readers, "and yet ye are not" (Morm. 8:35). He is prone to both fiery diatribes against the unbelieving and the avaricious (Morm. 8–9) and bouts of crippling self-doubt (Ether 12). His tone in the book of Ether is urgent, excitable, anxious. Yet he finds comfort in communion with his Lord. Bereft of companions, Moroni seeks intimate fellowship with Jesus, who, he reveals, "hath talked with me face to face…in plain humility" (Ether 12:39). Though the bleak wanderings of his life would seem to show little sign of divine providence, Moroni insists that God's miraculous love reverberates unabated through time and place. Every sentence he writes brims with his faith in the constancy of Jesus Christ's universal power to save.

a theological introduction

Like the book of Ether itself, the word *theology* may land like a lead balloon. It is somehow both too heavy and too light—heavy with doctrinaire jargon but all too light on the pressing issues of our lives. In a satirical scene near the end of the novel *Madame Bovary*, a priest and a pharmacist hold a vigil at the deathbed of the tragic Emma. All night the two men wrangle over arcane matters of theology, ignoring the bereaved household who shuffle by in search of human comfort and understanding. As they leave for breakfast, the priest sprinkles the room with holy water and the pharmacist pours a little chlorine water on top for good measure. So much for the spiritual edification of theology. One imagines Christ's rebuke: "Ye pay tithe of mint and anise and cummin, and have omitted the weightier matters of the law, judgment, mercy, and faith" (Matt. 23:23).

This theological introduction to the book of Ether, together with the other volumes in the series, works to shed the baggage that clings to this idea of theology. I leave to the pharmacist and priest all combat over cumin, any wrangle for the right answer. I look instead to Latter-day Saint scholar Francine Bennion's vision of theological investigation:

> It is not enough that theology be either rational or faith promoting. It must be both. It is not

enough that satisfying theology be mastered by a few expert scholars, teachers, and leaders. It must be comfortably carried by ordinary people. It is not enough that theology helps me to understand God. It must also help me to understand myself and my world.[3]

Bennion captures theology's responsibility to the mind and the heart, to the expert and the rookie, to the things of heaven and the things of earth. In the chapters that follow, readers may occasionally be challenged by the style and conventions of scholarly writing. Behind that challenge, however, lies my aspiration to a grounded theology that "help[s] me to understand myself and my world." Because this is an introductory volume, some worthy aims lie outside my scope. I will not undertake systematically to address every theme in the book of Ether, nor to do justice to its history of interpretation. I do not weigh in with doctrinal resolutions of, for instance, the several open questions surrounding the brother of Jared's visitation. I do not address many matters of politics and history, notably the recurrent theme of secret combinations. The approach I adopt here looks to scripture on its own terms and with interpretive resources drawn mostly from the Book of Mormon itself, seeking to discern its spiritual work and translate its call.

To be sure, there is nothing transparent about the interpretation of scripture, even when one sets aside the search for definitive answers and the external grids of meaning that must guide such a search. My basic method in this study is threefold: ① to make the best sense I can of the text's language and structures, ② to infer something of the writer's intent, and then ③ to press beyond plain sense and authorial intent to draw out emergent patterns of meaning at work in the passage. The first two stages rely on accurate description of what the text is saying and how it says it, an important goal to which I give my best effort. However, in the third stage I aim for something on top of accurate representation. Accurate representation, after all, demands faithfulness only to the words on the page—a necessary and rigorous starting place, to be sure! But scripture demands faithfulness to God. Scripture demands repentance. Theology's deeper fidelity to scripture lies not only in its accuracy but in its *agency*, by which I mean theology's power to amplify scripture's call to change our lives, its capacity to act on our desires with a portion of God's reflected love.

To accomplish these active ends of theology, I search the book of Ether for themes at the heart of religion as it is experienced by believers—existential questions about the nature of salvation, our access to Christ, and our own role in God's unfolding purposes. I look for moments when Moroni himself models a wrestle with God over the pages of a written text, when he brings the best of his creative and emotional energies to make something ready for God's touch. And I look for the ways in which the scripture takes on a power of its own, beyond Moroni's prophetic intent, to interact directly with its readers.

I begin the book at high altitude. In chapter 1, I consider Moroni's largest purposes and preoccupations as he prepares the book of Ether. As I've noted, Moroni orients himself toward modern readers of the Book of Mormon, whom he addresses as the Gentiles. He is deeply concerned about the spiritual fate of this people, whose vanity and unbelief he has prophetically foreseen. Without the covenants of Abraham and Moses promising salvation to Israel's scattered branches, how can the Gentiles repent and claim their salvation in Christ? He finds his answer in the experience of the brother of Jared, whose faith prepares him for an individual encounter with Christ equal in its saving power to the Lord's ministry among the Nephites. In chapter 2, I continue to trace the book's overarching exploration of faith. I focus on Moroni's extended comments in Ether 12 on faith and miracle, which I set in conversation with Nephi's teachings on Christ. I argue that Moroni and Nephi share a common worry and a common strategy as they seek to reach their respective readerships. From two prophets situated on opposite sides of Christ's visit to the Nephites, we learn that seeing the Savior is as much a question of *when* to look as where. In chapter 3, I reflect on the ethics of the editorial purposes I outline in the previous chapters. Moroni has a clear agenda for the book of Ether, and at times he overwrites Jaredite history and culture in order to convey his own priorities. I look to the Book of Mormon's own ethics of reading to evaluate Moroni's approach. Offering a new reading of the Jaredites' escape from linguistic confusion, I find that Moroni's treatment of the ancient Book of Ether models a living translation that invigorates rather than depletes scripture.

In chapter 4, I turn from Moroni's explicit purposes to the larger meanings that take shape in the book of Ether. I argue that the book is notable for its self-conscious investigation of the origins and nature of scripture itself. Returning to the brother of Jared's mountaintop experience, and connecting it to Moroni's famous reflections on weakness in chapter 12, I find in the sixteen small stones an innovative reception-centered theology of scripture. This approach gives each reader an individual role in bringing forth the divine dimension of sacred writ. Scripture shines with divine light when God touches its reader with grace and she in turn receives the book with charity. In the book's conclusion, I consider the vision of Ether in chapter 13 as a synthesis of Moroni's most urgent theological concerns. The prophecy of a New Jerusalem brings together the book's focus on expanding the circle of salvation in Christ, its ethical interest in indigenous peoples and ethnic relations within the chosen land, and its attention to the events of the last days. It shows that the renewal of all things is close at hand.

1

Moroni Considers the Salvation of the Gentiles

introduction

The book of Ether is marked by the conspicuous absence of the prophet for whom it is named. As we've seen, Moroni's voice breaks in regularly throughout the text, but Ether's personal voice is silent until the final verse. If we narrow our focus to the theologically rich chapters 3, 4, and 12, Moroni's predominance is even more pronounced. To begin to understand the text, then, we might first ask about its editor's intention. What is Moroni up to in the book of Ether? This approach is limited, to be sure, because there is so much at work in scripture beyond the conscious aims of its textual producers: the underlying influence of culture and genre, the experience of readers, and the constraints of human language and translation all play a role shaping scripture. And the ineffable inspiration of God brings it all to life. To introduce the basic elements of a scriptural book, however, it makes sense to start with the intentions of those who directly fashion its form.

In this chapter I address Moroni's largest themes, the lessons he most urgently wants to communicate to his readers. Moroni sees the Book of Mormon as a mirror for its readers, and he urges us to see our lives in its pages. Perhaps counterintuitively, his long immersion in Jaredite history turns his heart forward to the modern readers who will receive it. He insists that the Nephite and Jaredite histories, which risk being dismissed as a pair of dusty antiques, are alive with promises and warnings directly relevant to modern readers. Indeed, he sees a spiritual kinship between the ancient Jaredite people and the future Gentiles, both of whom are ethnic outsiders to the house of Israel. Because of this link, the remarkable faith of the brother of Jared becomes a guide to salvation in Christ for all who fall outside the chosen tribes. Faith is thus at the center of Moroni's theological vision. Faith makes salvation available to every soul, even to those souls who appear to be thrown by fate outside the reach of Christian teaching. Faith also promises the ultimate salvation of every people, provided that each group faithfully takes up its prophesied role in the last days. If they will not, the destruction of the Nephite and Jaredite peoples holds up a dark mirror to the future. From his privileged prophetic position high on the wall between past and future, Moroni is determined to do what he can to avert catastrophe.

Jaredites, Nephites, and Gentiles: a triangle of sacred history

What is Moroni's primary goal in his abridgement of the Book of Ether? This question received sustained attention in Grant Hardy's book *Understanding the Book of Mormon*.[1] Hardy argues that Moroni's abridgement of the twenty-four gold plates aims quite simply to transform the Jaredite text into Christian scripture. He shows that the Jaredite record in itself, without Moroni's interspersed comments, contains little material about Jesus Christ and the Christian gospel, beyond the passage in Ether 3:6–16 describing the brother of Jared's encounter with Christ. Surprising as this seems, other scholars have likewise suggested that Moroni

19

actively shapes the material he finds in the Book of Ether to emphasize Christian themes, both in his six inserted comments and, more subtly, in his abridgement of Jaredite history.[2] I follow this line of thought, and I start from the assumption that Moroni's mind is always present in the text, whether speaking directly or shaping the Jaredite story to highlight the meanings he finds most important. These meanings always center around Jesus Christ.

Moroni's first step in transforming the Book of Ether into Christian scripture, then, is to highlight any connection he sees between the Jaredite record and the Christian gospel preached among the Nephites. Moroni wants to persuade the reader that this ancient indigenous text, distinct from Nephite culture and religion, independently confirms the universal truth of the Christian revelation given to his people centuries before their extinction. Moroni wants, in short, to prove that "the God of the [Jaredites'] land...is Jesus Christ" (Ether 2:12). He shapes the story of the Jaredites to reveal the same divine hand that shapes Nephite history in his father's record. Their God is our God, Moroni asserts, and the lessons of their history are the lessons of ours. It follows from Moroni's careful parallel shaping of the two accounts that Jesus Christ, the Nephite Messiah, is the universal Savior, and salvation is available to every land and people—to the non-Abrahamic Jaredites no less than to the Nephite branch of the house of Jacob. Salvation is prepared "from the foundation of the world," and its inexhaustible power is available to all (Ether 4:19).

Moroni looks for confirmation of Nephite Christianity in his Christ-focused explanations of Jaredite scripture. The obvious first place for Moroni to train his connection-seeking eye is on the divine visitation of Jesus Christ to the brother of Jared. This showstopping passage, which combines brilliant storytelling and powerful symbolism, is an ideal text for Moroni to make spiritual connections between the two records. He takes pains to clarify that the Lord who appears on the mountaintop is the same Jesus Christ who visited the Nephites, "even after the manner and in the likeness of the same body even as he showed himself unto the Nephites. And he ministered unto him even as he ministered unto the Nephites" (Ether 3:17–18). Moroni uses the incident to illustrate a Nephite theology of faith developed by Alma, which teaches that powerful spiritual knowledge grows out of one's preliminary faith in the face of uncertainty (see Alma 32:21–29). Moroni offers the brother of Jared's mountaintop theophany to show that a personal encounter with God can transform faith into "perfect knowledge" (Ether 3:19–20). He explains that the brother of Jared obtained his encounter with Jesus Christ "because of [his]...exceeding faith" and later adds that likewise "it was by faith that Christ showed himself unto our fathers [the Nephites]" (Ether 3:9 and 12:7). For Moroni, the Jaredite experience confirms Nephite Christianity's emphasis on faith.

But Moroni wants to think more widely still, beyond the Jaredite and the Nephite peoples—both of which, after all, have been violently swept off the promised land, their only future contained in the book he writes. He wants to confirm the truth of the Christian gospel in the future, as well as the past, and this leads him to consider a third people, separated by time from the Nephites but connected by their shared place in the promised land. To the paired Jaredites and Nephites, Moroni adds the modern Gentiles at the time of the Book of Mormon's appearance. The triad of Jaredites, Nephites, and Gentiles becomes the basis for Moroni's historical and theological teaching in the book of Ether.

Moroni knows that the modern Gentiles will be the first readership of the record he is making. Without a community of his own to address, Moroni turns directly to his future readers. Neither the resistance of metal plates nor the passage of centuries will dampen the urgency of Moroni's voice: "And this cometh unto you, O ye Gentiles, that ye may know the decrees of God" (Ether 2:11). He will call the future to attention.

This kind of three-way thinking, between Nephites, Jaredites, and Gentiles, is different from the approach of the earlier Book of Mormon narrators, Nephi$_1$ and Mormon. These prophets are aware of a future readership, and they know of the Gentiles' crucial role to deliver the Book of Mormon to native peoples in the grand drama of the last days, but both remain largely focused on the value of their work for the remnant seed of Lehi$_1$.[3] Moroni, on the other hand, is aware of the Lehite remnant in the latter days, but this group appears only late in the book in a brief discussion of the New Jerusalem to be built by the seed of Joseph (Ether 13:1–12). Moroni reserves his most sustained theological interest for the modern Gentiles, not the modern Lamanites.

To his Gentile readers, Moroni addresses a series of comparisons between Jaredite and Nephite history that speaks directly to the modern spiritual condition. These three distinct peoples are shown to be linked by their individual migrations to the same "choice land" under the protection of the same "God of the land, who is Jesus Christ" (Ether 2:12). Moroni warns modern readers that they may suffer the same catastrophe that destroyed the Jaredites and the Nephites. He attributes this destruction to Satanic "secret combinations," a universal force of corruption opposite the universal promise of salvation in Christ (Ether 8:23–25). But he promises that the Gentiles may avoid this fate by repenting and serving God in the person of Jesus Christ, "who hath been manifested by the things which we have written [in the Nephite record]" (Ether 2:12). The embodied Christ who visited the Nephites is the same God who destroyed the ancient Jaredites and whose wrath hangs over the modern Gentiles if they refuse to learn from sacred history.

Moroni's focus on the Gentiles of the future likely reflects his long isolation from any rooted flesh-and-blood community, an absence that shifts his attention to the future destiny of the book he spends his life writing. He pursues a particular question about the Gentiles, perhaps sparked by a theological riddle in the Jaredite record. The Jaredites, like the Gentiles, are a non-Abrahamic people outside the covenant history of the house of Israel. These two groups test the saving scope of the Nephite and Abrahamic covenants. May those outside the covenant receive salvation? If so, on what basis rests the salvation of the non-Abrahamic? The Book of Ether provides a rich testing ground for Moroni to explore this previously unanswered theological problem.

Moroni as the Nephite minister to the Gentiles
From its early development, the Nephite theological tradition understands that the modern Gentiles will be central in the events of last days, as a force of deliverance or as an object of divine wrath. In his vision of 1 Nephi 13, Nephi₁ foresees the record of the Jews in the hands of the modern Gentiles and is assured that they can repent. In this knowledge, Nephi reads a fragment of the prophetic writings of Zenos as the scriptural basis for the salvation of non-Israelites, including the Gentiles: "Yea, and all the earth shall see the salvation of the Lord, saith the prophet; every nation, kindred, tongue and people shall be blessed" (1 Ne. 19:17).

Zenos's teaching echoes the language of the Abrahamic covenant—"In thy seed shall all the kindreds of the earth be blessed"—which is recorded in the brass plates and reiterated by Nephi₁ (1 Ne. 22:9). In line with the Abrahamic covenant, then, Nephi₁ bases his teachings of the universal salvation of all peoples in the Lord's covenant with a chosen people. But if the covenant is specific to one people, how is salvation universal? At the end of his record, Nephi₁ explains that the Lord's covenant is not constrained by ethnic boundaries but enabled by repentance and belief: "As many of the Gentiles as will repent are the covenant people of the Lord; and as many of the Jews as will not repent shall be cast off; for the Lord covenanteth with none save it be with them that repent and believe in his Son" (2 Ne. 30:2). This is a paradigm-shattering declaration, a seemingly radical dismantling of the Abrahamic and Mosaic covenants that are channeled through the house of Jacob (see Gen. 22:18; Ex. 19:3). But Nephi₁'s statement remains curiously unexplored by subsequent Book of Mormon prophets. Ethnic lineage cannot serve as the channel of God's covenant grace for those outside the house of Jacob, so what principle takes its place? It falls to Moroni to work out a theological principle for the salvation of those born outside the covenant.

Moroni discovers his answer in the brother of Jared's extraordinary faith. Jared's brother lives long before the covenant establishment of Israel, in a place remote from the sacred landscape of the patriarchs. He is decisively removed from Israelite covenant lineage and the great narratives of slavery and salvation, exile and deliverance, that inform Nephite religion. Yet his story is an archetype of salvation—salvation by *faith*. Much like Jesus's exclamation about the faithful centurion, "I have not found so great faith, no, not in Israel" (Luke 7:9), Moroni reads the brother of

Jared as a paragon of faith outside of covenant, of whom Christ may likewise exclaim, "never has man believed in me as thou hast" (Ether 3:15). The faith of the outsider becomes, ironically, the model for covenant insiders. The strength of this faith opens the way to salvation in Christ: "Because thou knowest these things ye are redeemed from the fall; therefore ye are brought back into my presence" (Ether 3:13). The brother of Jared's salvation occurs through faith alone, outside of birth-covenant. Building on this discovery, Moroni's characteristic triangulation between Jaredites, Nephites, and Gentiles suggests that faith opens the way to salvation for modern Gentiles, as well. Joseph Spencer observes exactly this theological idea at work in Moroni's portrayal of the brother of Jared as spiritually analogous to the Gentiles: "As a model for the similarly uncalled Gentiles, the brother of Jared displays a sort of non-Abrahamic faith that, if imitated by Gentiles generally, can result in 'the unfolding [of] all [of God's] revelations' (Ether 4:7)."[4] If the brother of Jared may be saved by faith despite his birth outside the biblical covenant, then so too may the Gentiles. The brother of Jared discovers a way to God routed not primarily through ethnic covenant but through the exercise of faith. Faith and covenant may be beautifully harmonized, of course, but Moroni's focus in the book of Ether is firmly on faith. 🖝

Readers familiar with the New Testament will note a number of connections between Moroni's concerns and the theology of the epistles of Paul. Both Moroni's and Paul's writings begin from the deliverance of one

🖝 Discussion of *covenant* is rare in the book of Ether. Moroni mentions *covenant* only twice, at Ether 4:15 and 13:11, both times in reference to the deliverance of Israel in the last days. The word never appears outside of Moroni's inserted comments, though the Lord does speak in a *covenantal* mode at Ether 1:42. Moroni never mentions *covenant* in connection with the Jaredites of the Gentiles.

ethnic group—for Moroni, the Nephites; for Paul, the Jewish disciples of Jesus—and show that salvation is extended beyond those boundaries. Moroni and Paul are urgently concerned with the Gentiles' acceptance of the Christian gospel first revealed in the Jewish contexts of the Book of Mormon and first-century Judea, respectively. Both Moroni and Paul are convinced that Christ's power to overcome death and hell through the resurrection is portable through time and place, not tied to one cultural context. Christ's power must be slotted into diverse societies, languages, and religious traditions. Moroni's use of the Jaredite tradition to show that the "God of the [Jaredites'] land...is Jesus Christ" (Ether 2:12) is like Paul's purpose at Mars Hill, where he preaches to the Athenians, drawing from their own poetic tradition, that their "unknown God" is, in truth, the universal Father manifest in the person of Jesus Christ (Acts 17:22–31). Moroni sees himself, like Paul, as a kind of minister to the Gentiles, and he takes it upon himself to universalize the local events of Christ's ministry among the Nephites.

Above all, Moroni and Paul both preach faith as the basis of salvation for those outside ethnic covenant and law. They arrive at this conclusion through similar scriptural methods: both reinterpret the tale of an ancient non-Christian hero to highlight his faith as the way to salvation. Where Moroni looks to the brother of Jared, Paul looks to Abraham. In Romans 4 and Galatians 3, Paul argues that Abraham, living before the law of Moses was given, must therefore have been justified by his faith, not by his adherence to Mosaic law. "For what saith the scripture? Abraham believed God, and it was counted unto him for righteousness...For the promise...was not to Abraham, or to his seed, through the law, but through the righteousness of faith" (Rom. 4:3, 13). Abraham becomes the spiritual father of all peoples saved in Christ outside of the covenant and the law, because his faith charts the course for their salvation: "Know ye therefore that they which are of faith, the same are the children of Abraham. And the scripture, foreseeing that God would justify the heathen through faith, preached before the gospel unto Abraham, saying, In thee shall all nations be blessed" (Gal. 3:7–9). Abraham and the brother of Jared are theological doubles, functioning in the visions of Paul and Moroni as exemplary spiritual fathers who reveal the salvation of the Gentiles by faith in Christ.

salvation for all

A subtle reversal in the expected sequence of the story of the brother of Jared in Ether 3 offers a kind of thought experiment for testing the scope of salvation in Christ. Recall that the brother of Jared is brought fully into the Lord's presence immediately after affirming the truth of the divine being whose finger and voice he has just witnessed: "I know that thou speakest the truth, for thou art a God of truth, and canst not lie" (Ether 3:12). At this declaration, the Lord shows himself to the brother of Jared and announces that his salvation has been accomplished: "Because thou knowest these things ye are redeemed from the fall; therefore ye are brought back into my presence" (verse 13). Notice, however, that it is only *after* his redemption that the brother of Jared learns the name of Jesus Christ. The Lord continues in the next verse, saying "Behold, I am he who was prepared from the foundation of the world to redeem my people. Behold, I am Jesus Christ. I am the Father and the Son" (verse 14). Under a strict reading of the order in which Moroni recounts the story, then, Jared's brother is redeemed before he learns the name, identity, and mission of his Savior. Yet Christ continues immediately, "In me shall all mankind have life, and that eternally, even they who shall believe on my name" (verse 14). How is it possible for the brother of Jared to exercise saving belief in a name he does not yet know?

That salvation comes by faith in Christ's name is a central Book of Mormon teaching. Prophets declare unambiguously that salvation comes through knowledge of and belief in the name of Jesus Christ. Mormon summarizes this central tenet of Nephite teaching, writing that "the gate of heaven is open unto all...who will believe on the name of Jesus Christ" (Hel. 3:28). Lehi₁ and Nephi₁ see in vision—and Jesus Christ himself reaffirms in his personal ministry to the Nephites—that the name of Jesus Christ will flow from people to people by way of the Bible and the Book of Mormon, so that both Jew and Gentile "may be brought to a knowledge of me, their Redeemer" (3 Ne. 16:4). King Benjamin declares that Christ "cometh unto his own, that salvation might come unto the children of men even through faith on his name" and emphasizes that there is "no other name given nor any other way nor means whereby salvation can come" (Mosiah 3:9, 17). Yet Ether 3, perhaps the most dramatic and personal account of salvation by faith in the entire Book of Mormon, tells a story in which the moment of redemption *precedes* formal knowledge of the name and identity of Jesus Christ.

It is possible, of course, that this puzzle is the result of a redaction error in the text. Perhaps Moroni—or Mosiah, or Ether, or the brother of Jared himself—simply reversed the sequence of events. A corrected version might clarify that the Lord introduces himself as Jesus Christ, the Messiah and incarnate son of God, *before* asking the brother of Jared for an affirmation of faith in verse 11 and revealing his full presence in verse 13. Moroni does not directly discuss the unexpected sequence of events. And whatever riddles the text may present, it leaves no doubt at all that Jesus Christ is the Redeemer and the author of the brother of Jared's salvation.

Still, though, it's likely that Moroni has reflected, at least implicitly, on the salvation of those who do not yet know the name Jesus Christ. We have seen how avidly he works to understand the basis of salvation for modern readers outside the covenant fold of Israel, Gentiles who are acquainted with the name of Christ but must be drawn into the covenant by their faith. Like Enos, whose hunger for the salvation of the human family ripples outward in widening rings, Moroni places his faith in a universal Christ, a redeemer of all. Moroni wanders for decades through Lamanite communities who have never known Christ—or who know him only as a superstition of their vanquished enemies. No missionary is on the way to plant the name of Jesus Christ. If there is a path to salvation for these souls, it will not be the straightforward pattern of evangelization → conversion → redemption that previous Nephite teaching has laid out. The brother of Jared's experience, as written, seems to reverse that order. It would be typical of Moroni's character to ponder this theological problem and seek answers in the Jaredite text before him.

Truth leads one to charity. Charity springs from Christ. All true things are Christ's. One may be stimulated to good works by truth in unexpected guises, but regardless of outward form, these verses suggest, it is the transformative power of Christ that acts on him: "I am the same that leadeth men to all good." This leaves open the possibility that a spiritually sensitive soul who has no acquaintance with the name of Christ or Christian teachings—or whose acquaintance has been trammeled by cultural or personal impediment— may nevertheless respond faithfully to Christ in other forms. To receive any good thing, to welcome the truth that calls us to charity, is to embrace Christ. This idea, at least, could account for the seemingly out-of-order salvation experience of Jared's brother, whose recognition of divine truth in the unexpected humility of "the finger of a man, like unto flesh and blood," yields faith sufficient to bring him into the Lord's saving presence (Ether 3:6). Recall that the declaration "thou art a God of truth" prompts Christ to bring the faithful man into his saving presence. Spirit-aided recognition of truth is the key to knowing Christ in the guise of "whatsoever thing" leads one to good. In this, Moroni may have glimpsed the hopeful availability of redemption for other humble souls who, unacquainted with the name of Christ, embrace "whatsoever" truth leads them to do good. All true things are Christ's.

This insight would surely give Moroni hope for the good souls to be found among the tides of humanity through which he travels, alone after the destruction of his people and his church. And it brings assurance to his readers—all of us who care for souls who do not or cannot confess Jesus Christ by that name, yet who respond with Christ's love to "whatsoever" true thing life places in their way. These may yet have access to his presence.

For Latter-day Saint readers, of course, the modern Restoration provides additional insights into the means of salvation for those who have not learned to confess the name of Jesus Christ. Current teachings about the postmortal instruction of the dead in the gospel of Jesus Christ, the continuation of human agency and spiritual transformation after death, and the practice of proxy ordinances lay out a clear path to salvation for those outside the formal Christian fold. Although these ideas were not revealed to Nephite prophets, the urgent questions to which they respond, questions about the scope and means of salvation, consumed Moroni. And perhaps there is much to be learned from Moroni precisely *because* of the limits of his knowledge. Operating under conditions like our own, conditions of incomplete understanding, Moroni wrings out the texts available to him to test the limits of salvation in Christ. Moroni's searching exploration and his innovative readings offer an example of profound scriptural theology. Read together, Moroni and the Prophet of the Restoration seem similarly restless with the theological limits they inherit. Both demand our consideration of the limitlessness of Christ's saving work. From the perspective of twenty-first century Saints, Moroni's boundless compassion for those outside his immediate experience and his penetrating interpretation of the Jaredite record are models for all.

salvation of peoples through faith

The brother of Jared is a thrilling example for individual readers contemplating the vitality of their personal faith. Elder Jeffrey R. Holland writes that the brother of Jared's "life and legacy to us have become synonymous with bold, consummate, perfect faith," and his theophany is "a remarkable doctrinal statement about the power of a mortal man's faith."[5] For Moroni, however, personal belief is only one dimension of faith. Faith is also the key to God's large-scale salvation of entire peoples. Through historical comparison between the Jaredites, the Nephites, and the modern Gentiles— three groups separated by time but successively occupying the same place—Moroni integrates the principle of faith into the grand narrative of world salvation that Nephi$_1$ and Christ himself previously taught. Moroni's reformulation of this drama, worked out in Ether 3, 4, and 12, sets a pattern for the communal redemption of societies: each group is given a divine message (whether book of scripture, prophetic tradition, or symbolic text) that, if faithfully received, calls forth the saving presence of Jesus Christ. The Jaredite people, through the brother of Jared, receive the sixteen stones, a symbol of God's word intended for the community as a whole, and are blessed with a redemptive visit from the premortal Christ (Ether 3:11–13).[6] Likewise, the righteous among the Nephites faithfully cherish the prophecies of Christ's coming, and subsequently "it was by faith that Christ showed himself unto our fathers, after he had risen from the dead" (Ether 12:7; see also Ether 3:17–18). Finally, the modern Gentiles are given the Book of Mormon itself, which, if faithfully received, will call forth the second coming, or the postmortal visitation of Jesus Christ (Ether 4:6–17). Channeling the voice of Christ, Moroni promises modern Gentiles that "in that day that they shall exercise faith in me, . . . even as the brother of Jared did, . . . then will I manifest unto them the things which the brother of Jared saw, even to the unfolding unto them all my revelations" (Ether 4:7).

This historical analogy between Jaredites, Nephites, and Gentiles, however, also contains a darker vision of the Gentiles' future. Yes, the Jaredites and the Nephites received the visitation of Christ, and so too the Gentiles may receive their own visitation and revelation when they "rend that veil of unbelief" and exercise the requisite faith (Ether 4:15). But a grim lesson lurks in the parallel extinctions of the Jaredites and the Nephites. The destruction of the Jaredites has long haunted Nephite historical consciousness, a stern reminder that their inheritance of the choice land is conditional. They do not possess the land by right or title but by the favor of God alone. The Jaredites were swept off the land when "the severity of the Lord fell upon them according to his judgments, which are just" (Omni 1:22). Their scattered bones make a charnel ground of the choice land.

To the Nephites, these bones are another kind of text, a grim death prophecy in which they read the failure of their own faith and the ethnic annihilation that will follow. The Nephite prophetic tradition thus unfolds in the knowledge of its own future end, and this knowledge imparts a complex dimension to its theology of atonement. Salvation, in the Book of Mormon, is bound up in the problems of time.[7]

The last bearers of this tradition, Mormon and Moroni, are eyewitnesses to the fulfillment of the death prophecy written in scattered bones. They see the Jaredite tale rewritten in the limbs of slaughtered Nephites left to "molder upon the land, and to crumble and to return to their mother earth" (Morm. 6:15). Moroni's lesson to the Gentiles sounds the alarm: "And this cometh unto you, O ye Gentiles, that ye may know the decrees of God—that ye may repent, and not continue in your iniquities until the fulness come, that ye may not bring down the fulness of the wrath of God upon you as the inhabitants of the land have hitherto done" (Ether 2:11). Moroni fears that the parallel visitations of the Jaredites, Nephites, and Gentiles, which he carefully embeds in a weave of correspondences, may be overwritten by their parallel extinctions. The psychological and cosmic stakes could not be higher for Moroni: if the Gentiles are not to become another grim book of bones inscribed on the choice land, they must be persuaded to receive the Book of Mormon faithfully and to set in motion the Second Coming of Christ.[8]

2

Faith after Christ

introduction

In chapter 1, we saw how Moroni uses the Jaredite record as raw material to work out a theology of salvation for those beyond the reach of the Israelite covenant and Mosaic law. Looking backward to the non-Israelite brother of Jared and his extraordinary faith, Moroni sees a template for the future salvation of the Gentiles. Both views, past and future, assure Moroni that the saving power of the Messiah is available in all times and in all places. The book of Ether is Moroni's historical "proof of concept" for the universal salvation promised in Christianity (see 3 Ne. 16). In chapter 2, I examine the finer-grained view of faith that Moroni offers in Ether 12, perhaps the best-known and most-loved chapter in the book of Ether. To do this, I put Moroni in conversation with Nephi. The two prophets bookend the Nephite record, and their ideas speak to one another across the centuries. Their teachings on salvation connect in surprising ways because each writes in a moment far distant from the visitation of Christ—Nephi some six hundred years before, and Moroni four hundred years after. Each prophet must persuade his audience to exercise faith in a long-absent Messiah. Moroni's formula for salvation, I'll suggest, is a complement and update to Nephi's theology. Both Moroni and Nephi find that the complexities of salvation by law or by faith are closely tied to the complexities of *time*. And each formulates his theology around an ingenious take on the era in which he and his readership abide, whether long before the arrival of the Messiah or long after. Side by side, these two visions offer a compelling double view on the timeliness of salvation.

At first thought, time may not seem like a question of theology. We take its constant passing for granted as the backdrop of our experience. But readers of scripture will often find themselves grappling with time as a central dimension of our relationship to God. Formal theologians debate whether God exists outside of time, and, if he does, how he can act within time. For Nephi and Moroni, a more pressing question is how humans can relate to God *through* and *across* and *within* time. Scripture often speaks to us from the past as a voice crying or whispering from the dust, as Isaiah and then Nephi put it (Isa. 29:4; 2 Ne. 27:9). To make sense of scripture, which preserves traces of human experience with God, we must take into account the workings of time, honoring the historical differences we find and yet somehow transcending that gap. Moroni and Nephi seem to worry that their readers will see the elapsing of time, future or past, as a barrier between themselves and Christ, like a distant shoreline receding on the horizon. We reach for a telescope, hoping to train our gaze on that faraway point. Instead, Moroni and Nephi teach that time itself is an access to Christ, not a barrier, if we look to it as a magnifying glass for now rather than a telescope to then. Time itself is made in the image of God, and looking deeply into the present moment allows us to see this divine dimension. Whatever our chronological relationship to the atonement, a spiritual eye sees Christ in all things.

Ether 12: Moroni's summary of salvation by faith

Moroni's most sustained exploration of salvation by faith occurs in Ether 12, a blend of historical example, scriptural explanation, and personal reflection. Moroni uses these blended elements to explore the related roles of faith and law for modern disciples seeking salvation in a Messiah who seems long past. The chapter opens with a snippet of the Jaredite prophet Ether's preaching that "by faith, all things are fulfilled" and that "hope cometh of faith" (Ether 12:3–4). The Jaredite people, however, reject Ether's teachings "because they saw them not" (verse 5). It seems they refuse to trust his word and demand additional confirmation on their own terms. Ironically, they fail to place faith in the prophet's teachings about faith. Their failure becomes Moroni's occasion for a lengthy discussion of Nephite sacred history, illustrating his thesis that salvation comes by faith. As with all of Moroni's writings in the Book of Mormon, salvation in Ether 12 is something quite simple: it is the blessed condition of abiding in the Lord's presence. Understanding *how* faith leaps barriers of time and space to place us in the presence of a long-ago Savior, however, requires some thought.

On one level, Ether 12 simply recaps the book's overall exploration of salvation for the Gentiles through faith, but draws mostly on Nephite experience rather than on the Jaredite record. Moroni again finds salvation in Christ for peoples outside the covenant and law, reasoning from the Nephite visitation that Christ "prepared a way that thereby others might be partakers of the heavenly gift" (Ether 12:8). He again addresses the Gentiles, drawing from Nephite experience to reassure them that "ye may also have hope, and be partakers of the gift, if ye will but have faith" (verse 9). And he again draws on the historical analogy that organizes his vision of the grand drama of salvation, comparing the faith-founded visits of Christ in the Americas to the Jaredites (verse 20) and the Nephites (verse 7), and promising the

Gentiles that the same double-edged fate—salvation or destruction—awaits them (verses 28, 35).

But in Ether 12, Moroni layers a new set of ideas, suggesting that he has a broader theological intent. He refers for the first time to the law of Moses and its fulfillment in Christ (verses 10–11). He introduces the language of the "heavenly gift" to describe, in relation to the law, the "more excellent way" of salvation in Christ, of abiding in divine presence (verses 8, 10–11). He discusses charity and grace as the substance of God's love and the basis for "a more excellent hope" (verses 32, 34). Above all, Moroni holds up the necessity of faith, which he arranges in an ordered relationship to the witness of salvation: "ye receive no witness until after the trial of your faith" (verse 6). He then catalogs eight scriptural episodes demonstrating that the power of Christ arrives only *after* the disciple exercises faith and hope, despite initially "see[ing] not" (verse 6). He carefully selects these instances from periods before, during, and after the visitation of the Messiah, noting that "all they who wrought miracles wrought them by faith, even those who were before Christ and also those who were after" (verse 16). The following are these episodes, in the order of their appearance in the chapter:

1. The visit of Christ to the Nephites (verse 7)
2. The reception of the law of Moses (verse 11)
3. A series of miracles and wonders from Nephite history, including Alma and Amulek's miraculous escape from prison (verse 13; see Alma 14:26–29)
4. Nephi$_2$ and Lehi$_4$'s miraculous escape from prison, resulting in the conversion of the Lamanites (verse 14; see Hel. 5:45)
5. Ammon's conversion of the Lamanites, likely the miraculous manifestations accompany-

ing the conversion of Lamoni's household (verse 15; see Alma 19)

6. Jesus Christ's promise to the three Nephite disciples that they would not taste death (verse 17; see 3 Ne. 28:7)

7. The brother of Jared's visitation and vision (verse 20; see Ether 3)

8. The promise to Nephite textual redactors that the Book of Mormon will come forth to the modern seed of Lehi₁ through the Gentiles (verse 22; see Enos 1:13)

This final item leads Moroni to a striking passage of personal reflection, in which he discusses his anxiety about the potential failure of the Book of Mormon to inspire faith among its Gentile readers. Such failure would frustrate not only their own salvation but the covenant redemption of the seed of Lehi₁ and indeed, as we have seen, the Second Coming of Christ himself. In a well-known passage, the Lord assures Moroni that the "weak things" of the Book of Mormon may "become strong" in his grace (Ether 12:27). Moroni is in turn comforted in the thought that the Lord will "give unto the Gentiles grace, that they might have charity" in their reception of the book (verse 36). In a narrative masterstroke, the episode culminates when Moroni reveals that, after his own psychological trial of faith laid bare on the page, he himself has received a witness of Jesus Christ comparable to that of the scriptural heroes just named. He reveals "that I have seen Jesus, and that he hath talked with me face to face, and that he told me in plain humility, even as a man telleth another in mine own language, concerning these things" (verse 39). Moroni's life and his theology cannot be separated. He experiences Christ's saving presence according to the pattern he discerns in the scriptures and then offers his own experience to the reader as another witness.

Brilliantly structured though it is, Ether 12 contains some curious twists. Why, for instance, cite the giving of the law of Moses as an example of faith? After all, Moroni has just offered faith as the means of salvation for those *outside the law*. What is the role of law in this context? And why focus so intently on the chronology of the witness coming "after" faith? The word *after* appears in this chapter eleven times, a drumbeat for the parade of heroes.

Nephi₁ and Moroni: looking forward, looking backward
I suggest that Moroni, writing at the conclusion of the Book of Mormon, emulates and responds to Nephi₁, his prophetic counterpart who stands across the pages at the book's opening. Each prophet uses his chronological position in relation to the coming of the Messiah—Nephi₁ "looking forward" and Moroni looking back "after"—as the basis for a distinctive theology of salvation. In different ways, they find that disciples in every historical moment may see and abide with Christ by turning *time itself* into a spiritual lens. Briefly consider Nephi₁'s teachings in 2 Nephi on looking forward to Christ.[1] Nephi₁ tries to explain his people's observance of the law of Moses given their knowledge of the gospel of Jesus Christ. If they know that salvation comes by Christ, why continue to keep the law? "Notwithstanding we believe in Christ, we keep the law of Moses, and look forward with steadfastness unto Christ, until the law shall be fulfilled. For, for this end was the law given" (2 Ne. 25:24). In other words, Nephi₁ sees no contradiction between keeping the law and believing in Christ because the law points toward its own fulfillment in Christ. In keeping the law of Moses, the Nephites are indeed "looking forward"

to the Messiah. Nephi$_1$'s phrase *look forward* re-echoes through the Book of Mormon as subsequent prophets adopt and adapt Nephi$_1$'s teaching.[2] On one level, the phrase may be read straightforwardly as a chronological description of the Nephites' relationship to Christ. They keep the law as they look ahead the six hundred years to the coming of Christ, the distant shore where he will fulfill the law by bringing it to its "end"—both its historical conclusion and its theological purpose (see 2 Ne. 11:4). Indeed, this is how some Nephite prophets, likely including Mormon, understood the teaching.[3]

Yet there's evidence that in the small-plates tradition there is something deeper at work in the phrase *look forward*. In 2 Nephi 11:4, Nephi$_1$ explains that the law was given to "typify" Christ—that is, to be a type or an image of Christ. The law proclaims the good gift of the gospel in its very structure. And it's not *only* the law that typifies Christ in this way. Nephi$_1$ adds that "all things which have been given of God from the beginning of the world, unto man, are the typifying of him" (2 Ne. 11:4). Nephi$_1$ teaches that *everything* given by God, all creation, contains some image of Christ. "Looking forward" to Christ, then, need not mean squinting beyond the queued centuries while awaiting a future time of fulfillment. More fundamentally, looking forward to Christ is a way of seeing the Christ-dimension in the here and now. The idea of "looking forward," in other words, is a metaphor that invokes the Nephites' chronological relationship to the atonement as a way of expressing a spiritual vision that seeks Christ in all things. It's clear that small-plates authors understand "looking forward" as something beyond a strictly chronological foresight. The record-keeper Jarom explains that the people were taught "the law of Moses, and the intent for which it was given; persuading them to look forward unto the Messiah, and *believe in him to come as though he already was*" (Jarom 1:11; emphasis mine). That they "look forward" to the Messiah "as though he already was" shows that looking forward is a spiritual, not a chronological, orientation. Even in the very moment of his ministry, it seems, disciples must still "look forward" to Christ.

Nephi₁ is concerned that his theology of "looking forward" may be misunderstood as a strictly chronological matter. After he explains in 2 Nephi 25 the harmony between the law of Moses and the gospel of Jesus Christ, he cautions that "after the law is fulfilled in Christi, . . . they need not harden their hearts against him when the law ought to be done away" (2 Ne. 25:27). In other words, Nephi₁ worries that when the law has fulfilled its typifying function and his people no longer "look forward" *chronologically* to the Messiah—when they must look backward after the event of Christ's visitation—they may also cease "looking forward" *spiritually* to find the image of Christ in all things. Without the law of Moses to open their spiritual eyes, they may become blind-hearted. This seems to be why he warns his people not to harden their hearts against Christ when the law is retired. Alas, the eventual spiritual shipwreck of the Nephites seems to bear out Nephi₁'s fears. After the deterioration of the gospel community established at Christ's coming, Nephite preaching never again succeeds in teaching the people to "look forward" to Christ *after* the fact.

It is precisely this conundrum that Moroni attempts to redress with his theology of salvation *after* faith in Ether 12. His own people lost, Moroni looks into the future and considers the situation of modern Gentiles. Will Nephi₁'s theology of "looking forward" to the Messiah reach the book's modern readers, who are even further removed from the distant shore of the atonement than the post-visitation Nephites? Where

Nephi$_1$'s problem is persuading his people that salvation in Christ is available long *before* the physical events of his atonement and resurrection, Moroni's problem is persuading modern readers that Christ's power still reverberates through creation long *after* those events are shrouded in historical time. Early in his writings, Mormon 9, Moroni shows emphatically that God is still a God of miracles and that human faith is the key to revealing the divine love always radiating through time and place. In Ether 12, Moroni returns to this theme but packages it in a new way by updating Nephi$_1$'s metaphor of "looking forward" to Christ. What does it mean to exercise faith in Christ *after* his coming?

Moroni answers this question by offering a different perspective on the law of Moses. He argues that "by faith was the law of Moses given" (Ether 12:11). Placing the reception of the law of Moses in a long list of miracles attested in scripture, Moroni puts the law in a new light. He sets aside the law's meaning as a type of Christ, which is Nephi$_1$'s interest. Instead, Moroni focuses on the extraordinary circumstances under which the law was given. Moroni may have in mind Moses's meetings with God atop Mount Sinai, another scriptural episode illustrating that the miraculous presence of God arrives *after* the exercise of faith: "For if there be no faith among the children of men God can do no miracle among them; wherefore, he showed not himself until after their faith" (Ether 12:12). Moroni may be referring to either a particular episode in which Moses's faith is tried or the general trial of the Israelites' faith in the wilderness. 🖝 Consider, however, the alternate possibility that Moroni

🖝 The faith of Moses is discussed at length in Hebrews 11, which bears many literary and structural similarities to Ether 12. Interestingly, however, the law of Moses is never mentioned in Hebrews 11. This leads me to believe that, whatever the nature of Ether 12's literary relationship to Hebrews 11, or lack thereof, its theological concerns are different and tied to distinctive elements of Nephite preaching.

has in mind the *Nephites'* reception of the law of Moses at Nephi₁'s retrieval of the brass plates from Laban (see 1 Ne. 4). After all, Nephi₁ prefaces that episode with his determination to "be faithful in keeping the commandments of the Lord" (1 Ne. 4:1) and later makes reference to his own encounter with Christ, noting of Isaiah's theophany that "he verily saw my Redeemer, even as I have seen him" (2 Ne. 11:2). If the story of Nephi₁'s reception of the law of Moses is intended here, the reference would fit well with Ether 12's focus on episodes in Nephite history that illustrate exceptional faith followed by a miracle of God's presence. Moroni's brevity makes it difficult to know which scriptural text he has in mind, but his intent is clear: to strengthen modern readers in their Christian faith long *after* the events of the atonement by promising the renewal of their divine witness.

Just as Nephi₁ plays with the phrase *look forward* to express two different meanings, Moroni draws on several different senses of the word *after*. He uses it to show the wondrous fruits of faith on both sides of Nephite history, "even those who were before Christ and also those who were after," reassuring modern readers that they too may witness miracles through faith, that their place in history is no disadvantage (Ether 12:16). And the phrase *until after* appears frequently to show a sequenced relationship between faith and miracle in the scriptural narratives he highlights: "neither at any time hath any wrought miracles until after their faith; wherefore they first believed in the Son of God" (verse 18; see also verses 6, 7, 12, and 17).

Moroni invokes an important third sense of the word *after*, which transcends its ordinary chronological or sequential sense. Like Nephi₁'s theology of "looking forward," Moroni's theology of the time after is not strictly a matter of ordered chronology; chronology simply provides him with a memorable hook for his idea. Noting the faith of ancient priests, Moroni writes that "it was by faith that they of old were called after the holy order of God" (verse 10). *After* here means "according to" or "in the way of": the faithful were called "according to" the pattern of the holy order of God. The word isn't intended to relate two things chronologically but instead to describe a kind of relation in which one thing properly harmonizes itself to another.

If we consider that Moroni has this third sense of the word in mind at some level throughout the chapter, a newly personal interpretation of the relationship between faith and miracle laid out there comes into view. In this sense, divine witness comes *after* faith, not because it occurs later in time but because the form in which God makes himself present is shaped by the faith of the individual to whom he responds. The nature of one's divine witness gives itself *after* the nature of her faithfulness. This idea is clear in Moroni's explanation that the mighty manifestations given to the brother of Jared follow from the mightiness of his faith: "For the brother of Jared said unto the mountain Zerin, Remove—and it was removed. And if he had not had faith it would not have moved; wherefore thou workest after men have faith" (Ether 12:30). In this verse and the next, describing Christ's self-revelation to disciples, the word *after* does not appear in the sequential phrase "until after," as it does earlier in the chapter. I believe that, here, Moroni activates the word's third meaning: Christ works *after*—harmonized with, attentive of, responsive to—the faith of his disciple. God manifests his power to his children, individually and collectively, in a form befitting the character of our faith.

My experience of God will take a different form than the brother of Jared's experience—and different too from my husband's, my parent's, or my child's—because the character of my faith is personal. Collectively, we should expect that the faith of modern Gentiles entrusted with the Book of Mormon—the present-day heirs of the Restoration—will call forth different miracles and different kinds of revelation than did peoples of the past, because our faith is shaped by and to our historical moment. But God's love still reverberates, no matter how long after the events of Christ's life. We encounter that power in moments of grace given *after* the character of our faith. This is Moroni's theology of faith and its aftereffect.

Nephi₁ perceives a risk of misinterpretation in his theology of looking forward, and there is a similar risk of misinterpretation in Moroni's theology of the time after. If it is interpreted in a strictly chronological sense, the idea that miracle follows faith can be misunderstood as a kind of crude causation—as if the ordered linking of faith→miracle means that faith demands or purchases the miraculous presence of God. Moroni takes pains to clarify that faith cannot "buy" a miracle in a spiritual tit-for-tat. This is why he frames salvation in Christ's presence as a *gift*, which by its nature is not caused or purchased. He assures the Gentiles that they too may be "partakers of the heavenly gift"—a gift that he soon names as "the gift of his Son" (Ether 12:8, 11). While the form in which the gift is given responds sensitively to the needs of the recipient's faith, it always remains a *gift* that is freely given and must be freely received—not a menu board from which the recipient chooses a preferred flavor of gelato. It's possible to mistake Moroni's teaching that divine witness comes (chronologically) "after the trial of your faith," together with his inference that "the Lord could not withhold anything from [the brother of Jared's] sight" because of his great faith, as endorsing efforts to compel the Lord to grant one's desires in return for extraordinary displays of faith (verses 6, 21). By framing salvation as a heavenly *gift*, however, Moroni discourages such an interpretation. Faith is intertwined with divine witness, but faith and witness must be offered and received unconditionally. God shows himself to those willing to receive the heavenly gift. But neither giver nor receiver of the divine witness may coerce the self-giving of the other. To do so would be to wreck the nature of the gift itself.

conversion in time

Nephi$_1$'s forward-looking theology and Moroni's after-facing theology bookend the Nephite record. Their ideas still speak to modern readers of scripture, who look for God by turning forward in time toward the Messiah's return and backward to praise God's saving hand in history. In all this turning, time itself gains a different quality, the unique *timeliness* of conversion—a word that means, at root, "to turn around." Every disciple knows the wrenching experience of desperately awaiting Christ's rescue and, in the same moment, gratefully remembering it. This peculiar turn forward and backward in a single gesture, which is impossible to plot on a chronological timeline, is often seen in the Book of Mormon's piercing psychological descriptions of the *experience* of salvation in Christ. The classic example is Alma's description of his experience of conversion as a *memory* of a *prophecy*, that is, both a "looking forward" and an "aftereffect": "I remembered also to have heard my father prophesy unto the people concerning the coming of one Jesus Christ" (Alma 36:17).[4] Moroni invokes a similar structure of feeling in Ether 12, at the turning point of his anxiety-wracked confession to the Lord that he fears the Book of Mormon will fail in its crucial mission. In relief, he writes that he "remembers" that the Lord will prepare "a house . . . in which man might have a more excellent hope" (Ether 12:32). In other words, Moroni expresses his feeling of deliverance as a *remembrance of hope for the future*—a spiritual reorientation, or conversion, simultaneously backward and forward that seems to break time itself wide open. Christ is to be found in these cracks of time.

If conversion is a new way of experiencing time as open, not locked, we can understand why hope is the companion of faith and love. Moroni confirms that we may be "partakers of the heavenly gift, . . . [and] hope for those things which [we] have not seen" (Ether 12:8). Nephi₁ exhorts us to "press forward with a steadfast-ness in Christ, having a perfect brightness of hope, and a love of God and of all men" (2 Ne. 31:20). It's no coincidence that these prophets, writing from dif-ferent moments in time and with different relation-ships to the law, eventually converge on hope. Hope is the Christian practice most closely bound up with time. At first blush, we might associate hope with the future, assuring ourselves and those we love that "it gets better" when we make it past the present dark-ness. Despite human propensity to pin hope on a bet-ter future, hope is always rooted in the broken-open present, where Christ is found. Recall that Nephi₁ and Moroni each ingeniously turns his *present* moment into a viewfinder for Christ. Nephi₁ makes it clear that "looking forward" to Christ—whether six hundred years before his coming or two thousand years after—means learning to see his divine love and power well-ing up *now*. Moroni teaches that to abide with Christ *after* our faith is to experience the gift of his presence *now*, receiving his miraculous love in forms as diverse as creation itself.

Hope in Christ does not lead the disciple to dizzying flights of fantasy about better times to come. Hope, as Ether teaches, is an anchor:

> Wherefore, whoso believeth in God might with surety hope for a better world, yea, even a place at the right hand of God, which hope cometh of faith, maketh an anchor to the souls of men, which would make them sure and steadfast, always abounding in good works, being led to glorify God. (Ether 12:4)

Hope makes the disciple sure and steadfast, planted in time rather than skating across its surface. To be steadfast is to be secure in one's place and moment, just as an anchor moors a ship to the ocean floor. The disciple's place, whatever her historical moment, is secured in the present. The end of Ether's sentence, with its talk of hope as the steadfast anchor, thus changes our understanding of its opening phrases in an important way. In light of hope's steadfastness, "whoso believeth in God might with surety hope for a better world"—in the here and now—"yea, even a place at the right hand of God"—*in this very moment* (verse 4).

This is a hard teaching for exhausted souls who toil and suffer, dreaming of escape to better worlds. Moroni himself must have felt marooned on a God-forsaken island of time. Spiritual outpourings of the past and the future greet him from the plates whenever he sets to work; the isolation and depravity of his world rush in whenever he looks up. Perhaps he is speaking to himself when he admonishes those who "have imagined up unto yourselves a god who can do no miracles" in the present, those who imagine that "all these things [have] passed" and then despise the desolate world that remains (Morm. 9:15). Perhaps it is himself he seeks to persuade that God's miraculous power of creation still breathes over the world. Perhaps it is he who must learn again and again that hope is rooted in this life.

Hope leads us to the sober, patient labor of good works. It comforts us in the groanings of the present. This is true whether we live long before, long after, or in between the comings of Christ, as Nephi$_1$ and Moroni testify. Every day may be the day of our salvation. Every second may be the Messiah's door. Every moment bears the image of Christ because time is the inexhaustible well of life.

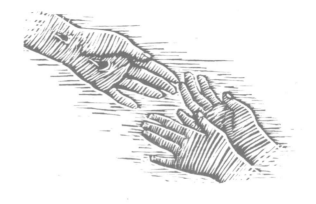

3

Among the Jaredite Ruins

introduction
In the previous two chapters, I've outlined Moroni's priorities as he reworks the Jaredite record. Like his father, Mormon, Moroni is an active editor who fashions the text to highlight important meanings. Moroni goes further than his father, however, by breaking into the Jaredite narrative to address modern readers directly.[1] Almost all passages in the book of Ether dealing with theological matters like salvation, theophany, and faith—heavily concentrated in chapters 3–5 and 12–13—are delivered in Moroni's personal voice, sometimes on the basis of only a faint resonance in the underlying Jaredite record.

As we've seen, Moroni's interests in the book of Ether are keenly focused on the spiritual condition of his modern Gentile readers, on their role in the redemption of the world's peoples, and especially on the place of the Book of Mormon itself in that grand drama. He concentrates on the power of faith and the spiritual transformation that occurs when one abides in the Lord. He is well versed in Nephite scripture and history, and he honors that tradition while processing the horrific fate of his people and interpreting their legacy in light of the future mission of the Book of Mormon. Above all, he wants to show that the divine man who ministered among the Nephite people, the long-prophesied Messiah and Lamb of God, is not merely the tribal deity of an obscure and extinct people. This Jesus Christ, Moroni urgently insists, is the universal Lord of all peoples, places, and times—the "God of the whole earth," as Christ himself puts it (3 Ne. 11:14). As Moroni sees it, the Jaredite record's value is its corroborating witness of Jesus Christ. Reading it, modern Gentiles will know that the force of Christ's self-sacrificial love reverberates forward and backward through history, transcending every ethnic covenant, law, and dispensation—for those whose faith allows them to sense it. 🖝

Moroni is *not* especially interested in the Jaredite record for its own sake. He passes over aspects of Jaredite experience that do not connect with Nephite experience. He shows little curiosity about the specifics of religious belief and practice. He has no comment on Jaredite society, culture, or politics, beyond the appearance of evil conspiracies for personal gain, which Moroni connects to Nephite secret combinations (Ether 8:20–21). Occasionally his indifference is puzzling, as in his silence on the Jaredite king Emer, who "saw the Son of Righteousness" (Ether 9:22). Given Moroni's sustained interest in human encounters with divine beings, his passing over this episode is strange. Where he does show interest in Jaredite experience—namely, the migration and theophany of the brother of Jared in chapters 1–4 and the prophecy of the prophet

🖝 Throughout this chapter, my intent is to reflect on the ethical meaning of Moroni's project as he understood it. As I've shown, Moroni's understanding of sacred history is organized around four groups who occupy the same land in successive configurations: the Jaredites anciently, the Nephites just prior to Moroni, the "Gentiles" in modernity, and the "remnant of the seed of Joseph" (Ether 13:6). Moroni does not speak of modern geographical boundaries, nor does he clarify the ethnic relationship between ancient peoples and modern populations. When I write about various lands and peoples in this chapter, I reflect theologically on Moroni's words; I do not advance any particular modern understanding of Book of Mormon geography or population genetics.

Ether about a holy city that will descend from heaven to the ancestral lands of the Jaredites in chapter 13—he does so because the material seems to confirm Nephite history or prophecy.

In this chapter, I reflect on ethical and interpretive issues in Moroni's overall project. We've seen what Moroni does with the book of Ether; it is also worth looking at the costs and strengths of his method. Is his intrusive editorial strategy justified within the Book of Mormon's own ethics of reading? What difference does it make that Moroni, unlike his predecessors, works with a Jaredite text originating outside the Nephite tradition?

sacred land and sacred scripture: an ethics of borrowing

When we read the book of Ether at face value, we observe more of Moroni's mind than of the Jaredites' self-understanding. The text is a bit like the scene in my autumn garden, where glossy oak leaves blanket the shrubs beneath: Moroni's perspective overlies the Jaredite record, revealing its basic shapes but hiding much of its original character. We read the book of Ether not for a transparent view into Jaredite experience but for the double view of a prophet striking sparks of Christ from an ancient text. Yet even this double view is insufficient, for Moroni's perspective is itself layered, incorporating his father's views on the Nephite tradition as well as elements of the brass plates and the traditions of the Old Testament—not to mention his integration of the mind of the book's modern translator, in chapter 5, and the language of the New Testament. The image of leaves blanketing a garden turns out to be too simple. Reading the book of Ether is more like hiking into a desert gorge, where band upon band of earth shows its own shade and texture beneath the high desert floor, whispering of massive dislocations in the past and future. The deeper we descend into book and canyon, the better we see how each successive layer—of rocky soil or of prophetic mind—refashions what came before and supports what comes next. We learn to read history's changes on the stone walls.

In the Nephite tradition that Moroni inherits, this image of a layered landscape littered with ruined remains is linked with scripture. The Nephites' connection to the promised land is, from the beginning, impermanent and conditional: Nephi$_1$ sees in vision the ruin of his people and a wave of Gentiles sweeping in to occupy the land. The Gentiles' tenancy is likewise conditional: if they prove unworthy of their gifts, they will be wiped off and replaced by the renewed remnant of the house of Israel. And each of these sweeping human tides comes bearing a book of scripture that it must preserve and transfer to the next, thereby unlocking a new phase of God's providential work in the land of promise. Those who fail to care for their book, like the Gentiles who deface and dismember the Bible, invite God's wrath.[2] The travails of the promised land, stained with blood and bones, are one with the travails of these holy books. Both are written on the scarred landscape, and their message to those who now inhabit the land is clear: all that you build up will pass away. As President Ezra Taft Benson wrote, "we remain here as tenants only."[3]

The Book of Ether is especially associated, in the Nephite tradition, with the idea of the promised land as a layered record of peoples, a slate wiped and rewritten over and over. The Nephites first learn of the Jaredites when Ammon hears about the Limhite explorers who, searching for the land of Zarahemla, find themselves in "a land which was covered with bones of men, and of beasts, and was also covered with ruins of buildings of every kind, having discovered a land which had been peopled with a people who were as numerous as the hosts of Israel" (Mosiah 8:8). The plates, discovered with a trove of ancient artifacts, carry the mystique— and the implicit warning—of an extinct indigenous people, their remains as rust-cankered as their records are unreadable. When the Jaredite record is brought to Mosiah for translation, the people seek interpretation not only of the plates but also of the ruined land and layered bones (Mosiah 8:12). The lost people and their mysterious record capture the Nephite imagination. The twenty-four Jaredite plates are transferred with the Nephite records through the centuries, but their content seems to have been unknown except as an ominous warning that God sweeps the wicked off the land (see Alma 37, when Alma transfers the Jaredite plates to Helaman).[4] The Jaredite plates, like the Jaredite ruins, mostly remain a mute mystery of an illegible indigenous past, crying from the dust for translation.

It's puzzling that Moroni, finally able to unfold the full meaning of the Jaredite record, seems incurious about the civilization for its own sake. As we've seen, he transforms the Book of Ether into an exploration and illustration of Nephite theology, from which the voice of the Jaredite prophet himself is virtually removed: there is no "I, Ether" in the book that bears his name. Moroni layers his perspective over the ancient record with all the subtlety of a Nephite highway built over Jaredite burial mounds. In one sense, this merely enacts the Book of Ether's figurative association with the ever-shifting layers of human geography in the promised land. But it also raises ethical questions. From a modern perspective, Moroni's translation could be seen as an ethnocentric appropriation of the original text, insensitive to the value of Jaredite experience in its own right. Scripture, to be sure, is often built upon the language and images of older scripture and need not be bound by the cautious conventions of textual scholarship. But the book of Ether foregrounds the ethical stakes of looking for Christ in somebody else's book. Moroni, unlike previous Nephite redactors, is putting his fingerprints on the sacred text of another people, not his own.

It is a thorny enterprise to impose modern ethical perspectives on ancient texts, no doubt. Yet Book of Mormon authors themselves reflect on the ethics of reading the borrowed sacred texts that crisscross the book's prophecies of world salvation. Questions about how to responsibly interpret a text are entangled with questions about how to respectfully treat a foreign people. Nephi₁ is the first to explore these issues, perhaps sensitized to the topic by his deep engagement with the prophecies of Isaiah, who gives the Gentiles a central role in the deliverance of the house of Israel and thus makes ethnic relations a focus of salvation history (see Isa. 49:22–23; 1 Ne. 21:22–23). Nephi₁ sees that his people fail to understand the value of Isaiah's prophecies because they do not understand its cultural context. He writes that "Isaiah spake many things which were hard for many of my people to understand; for they know not concerning the manner of prophesying among the Jews. For I, Nephi₁, have not taught them many things concerning the manner of the Jews" (2 Ne. 25:1–2). Nephi₁ himself is able to understand the words of Isaiah precisely because "I came out from Jerusalem, and mine eyes hath beheld the things of the Jews" (2 Ne. 25:5). Nephi₁'s lengthy explanations of Isaiah's prophecies are necessary in part to compensate for his people's lack of cultural understanding.

For Nephi₁, there is more at stake in these matters than responsible textual interpretation, as important as that is. The faithful borrowing of texts is bound up with ethical relationships between ethnic and religious groups. Nephi₁ lays out the issues in this impassioned condemnation of the modern Gentiles' future rejection of the Nephite record, worth quoting in full:

> But thus saith the Lord God: O fools, they shall have a Bible; and it shall proceed forth from the Jews, mine ancient covenant people. And what thank they the Jews for the Bible which they receive from them? Yea, what do the Gentiles mean? Do they remember the travails, and the labors, and the pains of the Jews, and their diligence unto me, in bringing forth salvation unto the Gentiles? O ye Gentiles, have ye remembered the Jews, mine ancient covenant people? Nay; but ye have cursed them, and have hated them, and have not sought to recover them. But behold, I will return all these things upon your own heads; for I the Lord have not forgotten my people. Thou fool, that shall say: A Bible, we have got a Bible, and we need no more Bible. Have ye obtained a Bible save it were by the Jews? (2 Ne. 29:4–6)

Here Nephi₁ connects the Gentiles' callous treatment of the sacred texts of the house of Israel—namely, the Gentiles' complacent appropriation of the Bible and their rejection of the Book of Mormon—with their persecution of the Jewish people themselves. The Gentiles both fail to appreciate the Jews' costly role in the Gentiles' own salvation by producing and preserving the Hebrew Bible and refuse to take up their reciprocal role in the Jews' salvation by accepting the Book of Mormon and presenting it to the remnant of Israel. They err egregiously, Nephi₁ suggests, by treating the Bible as their own scripture, with no appreciation of its earlier history: "A Bible, we have got a Bible." They fail to recognize that "their" Bible was *first* the Jews' book, and the Gentiles have received it only through Jewish sweat and blood. If the modern Gentiles properly understood that the Bible originated with the Jews, Nephi₁ implies, they would treat the Jews with honor and gratitude. To responsibly "occupy" the text of another people, Nephi₁ suggests, means to value their history and sacrifice.

Centuries later, Mormon shares Nephi₁'s compassion for the house of Israel in the face of the Gentiles' refusal to acknowledge their spiritual debt to the Jews. Reflecting on his reasons for recording the grim genocide of his people, Mormon writes of his intention that "a knowledge of these things must come unto the remnant of [the house of Lehi₁], and also unto the Gentiles, who the Lord hath said should scatter this people, and this people should be counted as naught among them. . . . And now behold, this I speak unto their seed, and also *to the Gentiles who have care for the house of Israel, that realize and know from whence their blessings come*" (Morm. 5:9–10; emphasis mine). Mormon evidently hopes that the Book of Mormon's witness of the horrific suffering of the Lehites will shock the conscience of modern readers, awakening them to their sins of persecution and setting before them their ethical responsibility to "care for the house of Israel." The Book of Mormon itself, the voice of the slain from the dust, is to be the chief agent of the Gentiles' ethical awakening to the indigenous inhabitants of their continent. Like Nephi₁, Mormon sees the ethical treatment of persecuted peoples as part and parcel with the ethical reading of their texts.

Moroni is likely familiar with Nephi₁ and Mormon's teachings. Moroni himself vigorously decries the interpretive mistreatment of sacred texts. In another passionate rebuke of modern Gentiles, Moroni asks,

"O ye wicked and perverse and stiffnecked people, why...have ye transfigured the holy word of God, that ye might bring damnation upon your souls?" (Morm. 8:33). He accuses them of "transfiguring" the scriptures, willfully misinterpreting the holy word to justify their pride, materialism, and neglect of the "the poor and the needy, the sick and the afflicted" (verse 37). Deliberate transfiguration of scripture, or interpretive faithlessness, is a symptom of the Gentiles' general faithlessness in the last days.

Overall, though, Moroni does not seem to share Nephi₁ and Mormon's keen awareness of the ethical dimensions of reading another people's sacred text. Perhaps his isolation from any ethnic community makes it difficult for him to understand the urgency of these questions for Nephi₁ and Mormon. In any case, Moroni does not express the gratitude, honor, and compassion for the Jaredites that his predecessors advocate in the delicate work of interpreting the religious text of another people. He is quick to interpret the Jaredite record in Nephite terms and use that interpretation to exhort the future readers, but he is rather slow to seek its meaning on its own terms. ☛ His "transfiguration" of the book of Ether does not approach the self-justifying defacement of a text that Nephi₁ and Mormon decry. Still, one can imagine an alternate treatment of the Book of Ether in which Moroni prioritizes *Jaredite* experience in his interpretation, in the way that Nephi₁ and Mormon urge modern readers to approach the

☛ Grant Hardy observes that "in a startling act of literary appropriation, [Moroni] Christianizes the Jaredite record." Hardy and other scholars note that no reference to Christ or Christian teachings appears in the underlying book of Ether. It is only in Moroni's direct editorial comments that discussion of the Christian gospel appears. The significant exception, of course, is the brother of Jared's mountaintop theophany, in which the incarnate Lord reveals his name as Jesus Christ. But these teachings seem to have been sealed with the brother of Jared's vision.[5]

Hebrew Bible with appreciation for Israelite experience. Respect for those who sacrificed much to produce and preserve a sacred text, they teach, is a form of honoring and caring for ethnic difference.

Modern readers can recognize that Moroni may have fallen short of his own tradition's ethical precepts without condemning his efforts. Moroni himself acknowledges that his own failings lead to certain weaknesses in the Book of Mormon (see Morm. 8:12). While he urges the reader not to condemn him, he does not reject personal criticism, and indeed he urges the reader to learn from his failings: "Condemn me not because of mine imperfection, neither my father, because of his imperfection, neither them who have written before him; but rather give thanks unto God that he hath made manifest unto you our imperfections, that ye may learn to be more wise than we have been" (Morm. 9:31). Indeed, Moroni's imperfections may be redeemed if his readers learn from his human shortcomings and resolve to treat people across ethnic lines, and their sacred texts, with respect and care.

This mutual care, faith, and respect between different identity groups is, in the Book of Mormon, far more than a social nicety or convention. The sacrifice of the Jews to produce and preserve the Hebrew Bible for modern Christians, the blood and suffering of the Jaredites and the Nephites to produce the witness of the Book of Mormon for modern readers, the care of these readers for the remaining inhabitants of the promised land, the transfer of the Book of Mormon from the Gentiles to the remnant of Israel in the Americas, the faith of this remnant which calls from heaven the New Jerusalem—these are the very means by which God enacts his saving purposes in the winding-up scenes of the world's history. Nothing less than the world's preparation for the renewed visitation of Jesus Christ is at stake.

translation or transfiguration of scripture?

Moroni's interpretive lens, while "transfiguring" the text from its original form in certain ways, also succeeds in "translating" its significance for modern readers and thereby allows it to reach into the world as a sacred text for a new era. As he writes in his first direct comment to readers, "This cometh unto you, O ye Gentiles, that ye may know the decrees of God" (Ether 2:11). The complex narrative voice of the book of Ether, the product of Moroni's Christianizing perspective layered on top of the other minds at work in the text, makes clear the necessity of translation, interpretation, and negotiation of scriptural meaning—in short, the necessity of an interpretive approach to scripture, and to language generally. Rather than assuming that the meaning of scripture is transparent and universal—or *wishing* that the pristine truth of scripture could escape the limitations of human language, which constantly requires interpretation and translation—Moroni's conceptual translation of Ether's record suggests something very different: *translation is precisely how scripture lives beyond its immediate context.* Like the three Nephites of Latter-day Saint lore, scripture is translated so that it can stay alive.

Though it may not be obvious, this understanding of interpretation as a vital spiritual practice is, in fact, implicit in the Jaredite experience itself. In the final analysis, Moroni's translation of the Book of Ether may be deeply faithful to the text's core meanings, even if it is incurious about its cultural contexts. In the final section of this chapter, I'll present a new way of understanding the foundational religious story of the Jaredites—one that sees a tragic misunderstanding at its heart but ultimately offers a redemptive view of scripture and language.

Moroni's translation leaves much unknown about Jaredite religious practice. Still, among many blank spaces, the absence of any Jaredite scriptural tradition is especially jarring. We know that early Jaredites had a textual tradition of some kind—or that later Jaredite culture projected it onto their earliest tales—because Moroni tells of the sinister "record which our fathers brought across the great deep," containing the secret oaths and combinations (Ether 8:9). After the brother of Jared is commanded to write and seal his vision, however, the book of Ether contains no subsequent reference to holy books. By contrast, Nephite culture is steeped in scripture: the Nephite record is littered with traces of an immense effort to obtain, preserve, write, translate, interpret, study, quote, and transfer scriptural texts. Translating scripture, discerning its patterns, and applying its meanings in new contexts is the beating heart of Nephite religion. Yet it is entirely absent from Jaredite experience. Why is this?

I suggest that the Jaredites' earliest stories foster a concept of language that hinders the development of a scriptural tradition like the Nephites'. The Jaredite migration from the old world to the promised land is often compared to the Lehite migration, and both are likened to the archetypal Israelite exodus. It's clear that the writers intended the reader to recognize these similarities, but there are important differences, as well. In particular, the nation-inaugurating migration of the Lehites is a deliverance from (potential) ethnic captivity, like the biblical Israelites' deliverance from Egypt. But the Jaredites escape from a very different danger: they flee the "confounding" of language at the great tower (Ether 1:33). The brother of Jared's first prayer to the Lord is a plea that his people be spared the corruption of their language (verse 35). His plea is granted, and the newly established Jaredite people depart from the land, likely assuming that they do so to preserve their linguistic purity. The Jaredites understand themselves to be the privileged possessors of a uniquely powerful language—a pure, perfect tongue that has escaped corruption and thus requires no translation, interpretation, or negotiation to maintain its vitality. Moroni seems to accept the Jaredite claim that their language derives a divine force from its purity, writing in awe—and envy—that the brother of Jared's writings "were mighty even as thou art, unto the overpowering of man to read them" (Ether 12:24).

Moroni agonizes that his people's writing, by contrast, must accommodate the ever-mutating linguistic drift of the Nephite language and lacks the pure, archaic force of the brother of Jared's; Nephite language has evolved to the point that "none other people knoweth our language," he writes (Morm. 9:34). Because of this, Nephite writers must revisit, rework, and retranslate their scriptures through both human effort and divine gift—not to mention deal with found scriptures written in unknown languages. But what if Moroni, like the Jaredites, has drawn the wrong conclusion about the Jaredite and Nephite languages? What if the Jaredites' assumption that their language needs no translation *is precisely what stifles the birth of a scriptural tradition?* And what if, conversely, the Nephites' laborious translation and negotiation of their sacred texts reflects not the weakness of a corrupt language but the lifeblood of a scriptural practice?

Perhaps the Jaredites' wish to escape the arduous, messy work of translation, however relatable, was misguided. They may have assumed that their escape from the babble at the great tower would preserve their sacred stories behind linguistic glass, transparent and secure from the confusion of the world. But in the end, it seems that scripture behind glass lacks the power to shape communities and souls. Had the Jaredites, like the Nephites, been forced to dust off and retranslate their sacred stories for every new generation, perhaps they would have found that the stories were not tarnished by the work but honed. And perhaps the presence of scripture as an active force in their collective spiritual life would have changed the course of their tragic history. Ultimately, the Jaredites, who arrived in the promised land with a pure and perfect language, fared worse than the Mulekites, who arrived without scripture and whose language consequently deteriorated (Omni 1:17). ☛ Sacred language benignly neglected is no better than sacred language carelessly abandoned.

I'm not suggesting, in this cautionary reading of the Jaredite experience, that we overcorrect, devaluing the original languages and contexts of scripture in a rush to make it relatable in the modern world. On the contrary, sensitivity to historical context is a crucial first step in understanding any text. But we should view as a gift, not a liability, scripture's high-maintenance demand that we grapple for its meaning over and over. There is a paradoxical value in scripture aging out of its original language and context. It is only in the wrestle to clothe an ancient text in a different language, to reframe its potential meanings for a new time or place, that the book grabs hold of the reader and gets under the skin. That our religious community's interpretation

☛ It's true, of course, that the Lehites, who arrive in the promised land with scripture and who assiduously preserve and cultivate their scriptural tradition, end up no less extinct than the Jaredites and the Mulekites. A vigorous scriptural culture is no guarantee against injustice, pride, and enmity.

of scripture changes over time is a sign of spiritual vitality, not decline. That we trudge through the same books of scripture on a never-ending four-year curriculum cycle should be, paradoxically, an opportunity for new vision, not tedium. Among the several channels of continuing revelation streaming between God and his people, we should include scripture itself—not as a glassed-in repository of original truth, but as a hands-on site of emergent intention. Our interpretive practice should attend to "translations" both conceptual and linguistic, as well as to originals. Scripture's center of gravity lies in the present, not in the past.

In the end, I am inclined to judge Moroni gently for his "transfiguration" of the book of Ether. We can learn caution from his hasty interpretive move to pave over the Jaredite text with a Christianizing gloss. We can honor his invitation to be "wiser than [he]" by treating other people's sacred texts with gratitude, sensitivity, and respect—and by amplifying that same gratitude and care in our interactions with the peoples from whom those texts were borrowed. Ultimately, though, scripture aims to act on its readers with an existential and spiritual force that no other kind of writing claims. For scripture to succeed in this aim, readers must encounter the sacred text as a living agent that can surprise them, challenge them, and speak directly to the experiential stakes of their life. Readers must open themselves to scripture as much as scripture opens itself to them. Moroni opens himself to Ether's record in this way. He reads the book urgently, looking not so much for answers as for raw materials to frame the questions that matter to him: does Christ's saving love still grace the Nephite homeland, many hundreds of years after the events of his visit? What is the meaning of the Nephite covenant, now that the Nephites have been swept off the land? How will the tide of Gentiles, soon to rush in, access the power of Christ in this place? Is he, Moroni, capable of crafting the Book of Mormon as soundly as the Jaredites craft their barges, so that it will succeed in its future mission? Moroni builds models of these questions from the Jaredite experience recorded in the Book of Ether, and he hands them through the ages to us, the modern readers of his book.

Contemporary readers may find that Moroni's questions do not move them with the same urgency that Moroni felt. The universal availability of grace to all ethnic groups is rarely questioned now, and ancient tribal distinctions between Jew and Gentile may feel irrelevant to a modern reader's personal experience. To keep the theological project of the book of Ether alive, we may need to translate it within contemporary issues and problems, just as Moroni did with the Jaredite record. Who are the contemporary "Jews and Gentiles," the insiders and outsiders of the current configuration of God's saving project? What are the social, temporal, or theological limits of our latter-day covenant of salvation, the sealing ordinance restored by Joseph Smith? Like Moroni, do we recognize those present limits, and do we work tirelessly to find new channels of living water for those outside? The book of Ether cannot supply all the answers to these theological questions. But in its pages Moroni models for us the method.

4

A Reader-Centered Theology of Scripture

introduction
How does writing become scripture? A string of words unspools, passing through a human mind to a human hand, and delivers up meaning encoded in written form. How does this everyday human process, used to produce everything from laundry lists to love letters, activate real forces of salvation and faith when the word becomes scripture? This is a question that haunts Moroni. He agonizes over the weakness of his writing. His poor dexterity, he fears, is inadequate to produce engraved plates, and his written expression insufficient to inspire anything but derision in potential readers. He looks at the plates and sees recalcitrant matter and fallible human minds. Will "these things," as he calls his textual work, succeed calling forth the cosmic events that he has seen in vision? There's an unfathomable gap, it seems, between what he labors to make and what it must accomplish in the minds and hearts of its readers.

In this chapter, I explore the brother of Jared's encounter with God through the sixteen stones he produces. The humble stones speak to Moroni's anxieties about the weakness of the "things" in which he and his father have invested their labor and passion. The narrative elements that Moroni sets in play as he contextualizes the story and guides its shape are connected to a distinctive Nephite theology of Christ. The story of the stones' illumination at the touch of the divine finger, I'll suggest, introduces a startling revision of the text's theism, or its understanding of God. This revision challenges the reader likewise to reconsider what she has assumed about divine power and about scripture as a vessel of that power. What is the power of weakness? What is the potential of things? What does it mean to see the "finger of the Lord" at work in scripture?

"When Ye Receive These Things":
scripture and its readers
Moroni adopts from Mormon a specific phrase to describe the fruits of their labor: *these things*. It's an unremarkable phrase, two common words strung together in the most ordinary way. In the course of the many hundreds of pages of text within the Book of Mormon, the phrase *these things* appears in a variety of contexts with different connotations. In the voices of Mormon and Moroni, however, the phrase consistently, though not exclusively, refers to the Book of Mormon itself. The following are a few representative examples:

- Mormon, ruminating on the future reception of his record, writes that "*these things* are written unto the remnant of the house of Jacob" (Morm. 5:12).
- Moroni, speaking of three witnesses prophetically envisioned, confirms that "they shall know of a surety that *these things* are true" (Ether 5:3).
- Moroni concludes the record with his well-known exhortation that "when ye shall re-

ceive *these things*, I would exhort you that
ye would ask God, the Eternal Father, in the
name of Christ, if *these things* are not true"
(Moro. 10:4).[1]

The phrase seems to function as a kind of shorthand for
Mormon and Moroni as they attempt to describe their
project and the work it will undertake in the world. ☞
But *the Book of Mormon* is a broad category and a big
book. What aspect of the Book of Mormon does the
phrase *these things* emphasize? We might assume that
these things are the teachings contained in the record,
or perhaps the physical record itself, which, after all,
occupied so much of the redactors' time and labor. But
Mormon and Moroni tend to use the term *words* to refer to teachings, and they most often refer to the physical record simply as *the plates* (see, for instance, Ether
5:1–3, where the terms *words*, *plates*, and *these things*
appear in quick succession, apparently with different
meanings).

In the American English of Joseph Smith's time,
"the primary sense of *thing* is that which comes, falls
or happens, like event."[2] The phrase *these things*,
then, when used in reference to the Book of Mormon
itself, allows us to see the book as a cluster of *events*,
of *things that happen*. How can a book be an event, or
many events? Note that, in each case cited previously,
as in many other instances of the phrase's appearance, the specific context is the future coming forth
of the Book of Mormon and its arrival in the hands of
its intended modern readers. Many hundreds of years
before it will be taken up by its first reader, the Book of
Mormon frequently imagines the moment of its own

☞ Jesus Christ also uses the phrase *these things* to refer specifically
to the Nephite record in 3 Nephi 21. Perhaps Mormon and Moroni
adopt this usage.

reception, whether faithful or faithless.[3] I suggest that this is what Mormon and Moroni mean when they so often refer to their work as "these things": the Book of Mormon distributed through millions of potential microevents, ordinary yet fraught with spiritual significance, wherein the Book of Mormon is sincerely received by a reader.

In this light, then, the Book of Mormon as scripture is as much an event as it is an object in itself. And when we look at it as an event instead of a self-contained object, its full character is revealed only in the moment it is received. Until then, the potential flowering of "these things" waits to be unlocked—and it is the reader, not the writer, who holds the key. Moroni's anxious imagining of the moment when mocking Gentiles take up the imperfect Book of Mormon prompts his famous discussion of strength and weakness in Ether 12. This passage is often read as a reassurance that personal failings may be overcome. But a closer look suggests that its primary context is the question of "scripturalization": how can an imperfect text, laboring under the limitations of human language, speak to readers with the power of scripture? The "weak things" that "become strong" are, it's clear, the Book of Mormon itself (Ether 12:27). And the weak things are made strong not in some general sense, but specifically "unto them"—that is, *unto the mocking Gentile readers*—when the Lord gives them grace and infuses their hearts with charity. Moroni comes to understand that the success or failure of the Book of Mormon *as an event* will be determined by the way it is received by its reader, not solely by the way it is constructed by its writer. In this Moroni finds comfort from a pervasive anxiety about his (in)ability to create living scripture: his role is simply to marshal the raw materials, the potential. It is up to the reader and the grace of God to breathe over the words and bring them into being as scripture. So the phrase *these things*, which suggests that the Book of Mormon's scriptural character lies in the events of its reception, points us toward a *reader-centered theology of scripture*.

For the Book of Mormon's first readers in early America, as for Moroni more than a thousand years earlier, questions about the character and creation of scripture commanded urgent consideration. What transforms a text into scripture? Could new scripture emerge and stand alongside the Bible with equal authority? Proponents of the "closed canon" argued that the Old and New Testaments stood as definitive and sufficient, even as others claimed that God continued to reveal truth through revelation.[4] Readers of the Book of Mormon would have found that the book, with its vigorous claims to a scriptural authority that complemented the Bible's, weighed in on several of these questions. The Book of Mormon implicitly denies that scripture is defined by any of the following:

- the infallibility of its writers, because human error is regularly acknowledged (Morm. 9:31);
- its comprehensive or sufficient character, because the book itself promises a flood of additional scripture (2 Ne. 29:12–13); or
- the ecclesiastical authority of an existing church, because the publication of the Book of Mormon preceded the organization of The Church of Jesus Christ of Latter-day Saints.[5]

Instead, the Book of Mormon taught its early readers, as it teaches readers today, that a text becomes scripture in the hands of humble, receptive readers who are moved upon by the Lord or his Spirit: then will "weak things become strong unto them" (Ether 12:27). Moroni shifts the locus of scriptural authority away from the prestige of a sacred text's writers, its religious institution, or its monumental self-sufficiency. As one scholar puts it, "the solution to Moroni's conundrum is not more powerful, Spirit-infused writing, but rather a new type of reading characterized by faith and charity."[6] Moroni's theology of scripture looks more toward *readership* to establish scriptural authority than it does toward *authorship*: the author's work is merely to nurture the scriptural embryo into written form, while the reader completes its final transformation into scripture in the moment of sincere encounter. A reception theory of scripture treats scripture less as an established deposit of truth certified by "author"-ity and more as a field of potential ready for communities of readers to unlock its meaning and power.

"Behold These Things":
the shining forth of the Book of Mormon

If one is willing to entertain my suggestion that the phrase *these things* alludes, for Mormon and Moroni, to the Book of Mormon itself, then the third chapter of Ether, one of the most familiar portions of the book, takes on new meaning. In Ether 2 and 3, Moroni recounts the brother of Jared's efforts to solve several practical problems that arise as he attempts to build the sea vessels that will transport his people to a choice land. When Jared's brother inquires about the lack of light, the Lord asks him to propose a solution. In response, he produces, by a process described in the text only as being "molten out of a rock," sixteen small burnished stones (Ether 3:1). He approaches the Lord on a mountaintop and petitions him to "touch these stones, O Lord, with thy finger" (verse 4). The Lord consents to the request and touches each stone in turn, kindling in each an internal light that "caused stones to shine in darkness" (Ether 6:3). Staggered at the sight of the finger of the Lord, Jared's brother is then granted a full vision of the divine body of Christ.

The story of the shining stones is one of the most memorable and beloved in the Book of Mormon, with its finely crafted literary shape, its evocative symbolic images, and its spectacular narrative payoff at the protagonist's encounter with God. It is frequently invoked to explore themes of faith, divine power, and the incarnate Jesus Christ. Elder Jeffrey R. Holland advanced an influential interpretation that reads the brother of Jared's experience as a test of faith and an exemplary exercise of human agency in alignment with divine will.[7] The story lends itself readily to this reading and others.

Now consider placing the Jaredite theophany in the context of Moroni's persistent anxiety about the sufficiency of the scripture he is making, "these things" he is trying to bear across the gap between inert object and living word. Just a few chapters previously, Moroni concludes his father's record in Mormon 9 with a discussion explicitly identifying "these things" as the Book of Mormon (9:35–36). This meaning echoes at the climax of the sixteen stones narrative. Jared's brother approaches the Lord, cringing but courageous, to present the stones he has made and to request the Lord's illuminating touch.

> O Lord, look upon me in pity, and turn away thine anger from this thy people, and suffer not that they shall go forth across this raging deep in darkness; but behold these things which I have molten out of the rock. (Ether 3:3; emphasis mine)

In his reading of the story, Elder Holland notes the phrase *these things* and finds in it the protagonist's "moment of genuine humility."[8] The brother of Jared's evident anxiety at the imperfection of his stony offering echoes Moroni's own persistent worries about "the imperfections which are in" the record he prepares (Morm. 8:12). The image of Jared's brother offering his sixteen small stones to the Lord's illuminating touch prefigures Moroni himself offering up the Book of Mormon, the "weak things" that will "become strong unto" those who will see its light (Ether 12:27). Both Jared's brother and Moroni have full knowledge of the offering's flaws, but they hope that it might yet scintillate.☞ No doubt the modern translator and the scribe of the record, Joseph Smith and Oliver Cowdery, also heard their own fears and hopes expressed in the story as they wrestled Moroni's redaction into English prose; the book of Ether is notable for its awareness of that modern translator (see Ether 5).

The paired figures of Jared's brother and Moroni offer their imperfect effort to the Lord, who touches it with divine grace. In both cases, the transformative power of God's touch is represented strikingly in the image of light shining in darkness. Jared's brother petitions "that [the stones] may shine forth in darkness" (Ether 3:4). When placed in the vessels, they function precisely as hoped: "And thus the Lord caused stones to shine in darkness, to give light unto men, women, and children, that they might not cross the great waters in darkness" (Ether 6:3). Twice in these early chapters of Ether, then, Moroni describes the stones as "shin[ing] forth in darkness." This language is linked

---

☞ Notably, the original Book of Mormon as apparently conceived by Mormon and Moroni was composed of sixteen individual books, the same number of stones produced by Jared's brother. Had a complete original Book of Mormon manuscript been produced, it would have contained the book of Lehi in addition to the fifteen extant books. This may further strengthen the connection between the stones and the scripture.

79

to a discussion several chapters earlier, in which Moroni prophetically imagines the coming forth of the Book of Mormon as scripture for a modern milieu:

> [I]t shall be brought out of darkness unto light, according to the word of God; yea, it shall be brought out of the earth, and *it shall shine forth out of darkness*, and come unto the knowledge of the people; and it shall be done by the power of God. (Morm. 8:16; emphasis mine)

The image of an object shining forth in darkness by the power of God is unusual in the Book of Mormon, appearing only in reference to the stones, the Book of Mormon, and, intriguingly, the mysterious "Gazelem" stone mentioned by Alma (see Alma 37:23). The connection between the glowing stones and the shining scripture goes deep. Like the stones, the Book of Mormon— whether considered as a set of metal plates or as an ancestral "voice...crying from the dust" (2 Ne. 33:13)— emerges as a fragment of earth, waiting in a dark elemental earthiness until brought to light by the labor of human hands and offered up to the Lord. Neither Moroni nor Jared's brother is able to expunge the traces of earthy origin and human manufacture in his offering to the Lord, and this appears to be both the source of anxiety and the occasion of faith.

When the brother of Jared's shining stones are likened to Moroni's understanding of sacred texts, we better understand how God is involved in their production. Previously I proposed a reader-centered idea of scripture, based in the Book of Mormon's frequent imagining of the moment when it is taken up by a reader. One might object that such a theory leaves little space for divine involvement, as if the term *scripture* might be stretched to include any favorite book beloved by a reader. When the Jaredite stones are seen as a symbol of scripture's production, however, it becomes clear that the Book of Mormon will countenance no "unfaithed" or reductively naturalistic account of its emergence. The book demands of its readers faith in God's sanctifying touch, the grace that brings forth scripture from the stuff of language. Moroni returns to this idea in Ether 12. Recall his discouragement as he imagines future readers heaping scorn upon his stumbling efforts to wrestle sacred ideas into language. The Lord promises that *he* will make these weak things strong—not by touching Moroni with mightiness in writing, but by touching future readers with "grace, that they might have charity" (Ether 12:36). The Lord accomplishes a text's final transformation into scripture after the author has wrestled ideas into language—after the stones have been molten—at the very moment a reader takes it up. If we follow Moroni's reception-centered idea of scripture, the true "coming forth" of the Book of Mormon occurs whenever a sincere reader opens the book with real intent. Any account of its emergence as a discrete, one-off historical event—whether miraculous or naturalistic—fails to grasp Moroni's brilliant reframing of scripture. The Book of Mormon comes into the world anew every time a reader cracks its cover and receives the grace shining from its pages.

the finger of the lord: divine weakness
The image of the finger of God that appears so dramatically in the story of Jared's brother is worth exploring in more depth, because it captures something subtle but decisive about faith and scripture, two central themes in the book of Ether. On one level, the appearance of the divine finger adds support for the connection I've proposed between the brother of Jared's stones and the Book of Mormon itself, the work Moroni lifts to the

Lord for divine illumination. The image of God's finger appears only twice in the Book of Mormon: in the story of the sixteen stones, and in Amulek's reference to the unknown Aminadi, "who interpreted the writing which was upon the wall of the temple, which was written by the finger of God" (Alma 10:2). In the Old Testament, the finger of God appears at Mount Sinai, when Moses presents the stone tablets on which the ten commandments are "written with the finger of God" (Ex. 31:18). And the Gospel of John, perhaps in unstated reference to the finger of God on Sinai, depicts Jesus "with his finger [writing] on the ground" when the woman taken in adultery is brought to him (John 8:6). In the Old and New Testaments, then, the image of the finger of God is relatively unusual and, when it does appear, is almost always associated with divine writing. The sixteen small stones, themselves touched by the finger of the Lord, thus have important symbolic connections to divine writing and scripture.

To my mind, though, the image of the Lord's finger points toward a new idea about divine power in the episode of the sixteen stones, an idea that seems at first to puzzle and then to intrigue Moroni, and to which he subsequently returns as he grapples with the meaning of the Jaredites' record. Readers of scripture recognize that the "hand of the Lord" is a relatively common scriptural metaphor for God's power, his miraculous work in human history, and his providential intention to deliver his people and chastise the wicked. But here, in the story of the sixteen small stones, it's not the Lord's hand we see at work. It's his finger. The symbolic differences between the two images, the hand and the finger, change our understanding of the brother of Jared's encounter with God. I intend in this discussion, which will become rather technical in its narrative exposition, to model the kind of creative engagement the Book of Mormon asks of its readers. When readers pause to savor the images—even the grammar!—that a scriptural writer has chosen to express his meaning, they bring to bear the consecrated attention and faith that calls scripture to life.

What is at stake in the difference between hand and finger? The hand is strong and capable. The hand grasps, reaches, and strikes. With the aid of its fingers and the arm to which it is joined, the hand carries out the intention of the body and mind. The scriptures use the metaphor of God's hand in all these ways. Consider how Moroni employs the image in the first verse of the book of Ether, where he gives the reader a bleak preview of the Jaredites, who were "destroyed by the hand of the Lord upon the face of this north country" (Ether 1:1). Here Moroni uses the metaphor of the Lord's hand to convey divine strength. The hand of the Lord, according to Moroni's meaning here, effectively carries out divine intention by reaching into human history and manipulating natural and human forces to bring to pass his providential judgment.

Reflect, in contrast, on the function of a finger. A single finger is small. In itself, and compared to the capabilities of an entire hand, an individual finger is not formidable or dexterous. Its power to grasp, coerce, or strike is unimpressive. A finger is inherently interdependent with its co-digits. Yet a finger is well suited for pointing and conveying other nonverbal communication. A finger is capable of astonishing feats of fine-motor manipulation, especially when used in concert with its fellows. A finger is best used for small-scale action that calls for more gentleness than force, more care than coercion, and more patience than strength.

In this light, we might read the finger of the Lord as a symbol of what Paul calls "the weakness of God" (1 Cor. 1:25). For Paul, and perhaps for Moroni, to invoke the weakness of God is a deliberate gambit to disorient those who, for good reason, venerate God for his power and triumph. The message of the gospel, by contrast, is that God's nature is revealed most fully in Christ crucified—the God who voluntarily *relinquishes* all "control or dominion or compulsion" (D&C 121:37). The weakness of God in Christ should not be mistaken for enervation or inactivity. The "weak force" of divinity is *force* (without force) and *power* (without power). It is influence without coercion, effect without domination. It is persuasion, long-suffering, gentleness, meekness, and love unfeigned (D&C 121:41).

When we see the Lord's finger as a figure for the weakness of God, a curious wrinkle in the narrative at the beginning of Ether 3 yields new meaning. In verse 4, Jared's brother has climbed the mountain and presented the stones, and now begs the Lord to "touch these stones, O Lord, with thy finger." Yet when the Lord responds, touching the stones in precisely the way Jared's brother has suggested, we're told that he collapses, "struck with fear" (verse 6). Why would he be so afraid, when the Lord has only acted as he expected? The text supplies one possible explanation, but to my mind it's both psychologically unconvincing and grammatically problematic. Jared's brother is reported to explain, in response to the Lord's rather puzzled inquiry, that "I saw the finger of the Lord, and I feared lest he should smite me" (verse 8). The suggestion that he feared physical harm seems ill-fitted to both his observation—as noted previously, fingers are not suggestive of violent action—and his behavior immediately prior, which suggests humble trust in the Lord. In addition, there's a strange grammatical glitch at precisely this point: Jared's brother temporarily begins to address the Lord in the third person, whereas immediately before and after he speaks to the Lord in the second-person address appropriate for conversation. These odd psychological and narrative discontinuities suggest some sort of redaction or editorial error in the transmission of the text, and they spur the reader to look beyond the surface.

Later, indeed, Moroni offers another explanation for the brother of Jared's unexpected shock or dismay at the sight of the Lord's finger: "he saw the finger of Jesus, which, when he saw, he fell with fear; for he knew that it was the finger of the Lord" (verse 19). That the brother of Jared comes to the mountaintop with a general anthropomorphic understanding of God is clear in his request that the Lord extend his finger. What shocks him, then, can't be the fact that the Lord possesses a finger. It seems rather to be that the finger is "as the finger of a man, like unto flesh and blood" (verse 6). Jared's brother may have expected the finger of a divine being to be massive and physically awesome. Instead, he sees a human-sized finger ordinary in its size and strength. It seems to be the incarnation of Jesus—the revelation of the Lord's human form—that so stuns Jared's brother. I suggest that it is precisely before the *weakness* of God in Christ, not God's mighty strength, that Jared's brother collapses.

Consider that Jared's brother faces an arduous seaborne migration to an unknown land. In the rugged design of the barges, meant to withstand prolonged battery and deluge, he begins to understand the dangers ahead. Yet the Lord has promised to protect the Jaredite band, and Jared's brother has staked everything on that promise. He quite naturally expects that his is a mighty Lord, able to control the seas and defeat the monsters of the deep in order to deliver the Jaredites safely to the land of promise. Imagine his alarm when the Lord offers instead a human-scale finger, weak and humble as his own. Perhaps, indeed, the Lord's finger is injured and raw; Moroni notes that the Lord shows himself in "the same body even as he showed himself unto the Nephites" (verse 17). The ravages of the crucifixion may be evident in the Lord's flesh. Is this weak, possibly mangled finger able to quell the waves and stay the monsters? When we suppose that the brother of Jared's shock reflects his dawning understanding of divine *weakness*, not divine strength, the quality of his faith becomes clear.

For Moroni, the lesson of the Jaredite theophany for the latter-day Gentiles, his principal audience, is the extraordinary faith of Jared's brother, faith that enabled and infused the knowledge of Christ's nature he gained during his mountaintop encounter. To have confidence in a mighty Lord of Hosts is one thing; to trust the saving power of a God incarnate and wounded, a Lord who reveals himself in weakness, requires the eye of faith. Great power here looks small. This is the faith of Jared's brother: "We know that thou art able to show forth great power, *which looks small unto the understanding of men*" (verse 5; emphasis mine). It is this kind of faith—faith in the finger of the Lord, faith in the apparent smallness and weakness of God in Christ—that Moroni specifically recommends to his latter-day readers, prophesying that when the Gentiles "shall exercise faith in me ... even as the brother of Jared did, . . . then will I manifest unto them the things which the brother of Jared saw" (Ether 4:7). For all the dizzying scope of the vision that concludes his mountaintop theophany, the first *thing* in which Jared's brother exercises faith is a simple finger.

To do justice to a theology of the weakness of God would require an entire book in itself.[9] I will simply note here the implications for Moroni's understanding of scripture, which I've traced through this chapter. Moroni builds into his narrative a link between the brother of Jared's sixteen stones and the Book of Mormon itself. If this is the case, the stones' illumination at the Lord's touch may be read as the divine light God kindles within the imperfect textual offering of Mormon and Moroni, catalyzing its transformation from inert language into living scripture at each moment of its coming forth in the heart and mind of a reader. And if it is the Lord's finger—a symbol of the weakness of God—that illuminates scripture, we would expect to see God's power at work in scripture in small and humble ways, rather than in overwhelming or conclusive displays. Moroni's theology of scripture steers us away from theologies that would exalt the divinity of scripture as inerrant, unassailable, over-certain, and conclusive. For Moroni, scripture is hidden and weak, struggling and erring—but it shines forth in darkness nonetheless.

It's a curious feature of the Book of Mormon that, despite its extensive interest in miracles *and* its extensive reflection on its own future emergence into the world, it never describes its own coming forth as "miraculous." Believing readers of the book, myself included, rightly marvel at the divine events leading to its appearance and the remarkable pace and coordination with which Joseph Smith and his scribes translated the book. But the book itself, strikingly, does not cast its own emergence in terms of the overwhelmingly miraculous or the impressive. It instead dwells on its own plainness, its weakness, and the riskiness of the moment when the finger of the Lord illuminates the book in the hands of a potential reader. God's promise is that the light will not fail. It will "shine in darkness, to give light unto men, women, and children, that they might not cross the great waters in darkness" (Ether 6:3).

First person accounts of the plates include a sealed portion. One witness, David Witmer, described the sealed portion as "solid to [his] view" and "the leaves were so securely bound together that it was impossible to separate them." See Kirk B. Henrichsen, "How Witnesses Described the 'Gold Plates,'" *Journal of Book of Mormon Studies*, 10:1 (2001).

Conclusion

Just before its bleak curtain falls on the Jaredite chronicle, the book of Ether offers one last glimpse of the future. The view differs in surprising ways from what readers have come to expect of this text. The great vision of Ether, retold by Moroni in Ether 13, turns from the history of a particular people, the Jaredites, to the history of a particular *place*. The vision opens on the cosmic beginning, as the waters of creation recede from the face of the earth. God sets apart one corner of the earth as a "choice land above all other lands, a chosen land of the Lord" (Ether 13:2). The vision of Ether begins as the story of a chosen land, not a chosen clan. Ether foresees a sweep of events that will usher the choice land into the fullness of its purpose. As the vision unfolds, human stewards enter to assist in the dramatic winding-up scenes of the world—but not, we're told, Ether's own people. The remaining descendants of Sariah and Lehi$_1$, called the "remnant of the seed of Joseph" in the text, build a sacred city in the chosen land, a New Jerusalem that rises as the counterpart of the ancient city after which it is named. The Jerusalems, old and new, will harbor gathered Israel, washed in the blood of the Lamb, and their rising will herald the sacred time when "all things have become new" (verse 9).

The flavor of Ether's prophecy in chapter 13 departs sharply from Moroni's previous reflections on the future. The modern Gentiles, Moroni's ever-present preoccupation, do not appear in the vision of Ether, which focuses instead on the indigenous "seed of Joseph." ☞ Ether's vision introduces vivid apocalyptic imagery, including the blood of the Lamb and the white garments of the faithful, which is otherwise absent from the book (though present in earlier Nephite tradition and familiar to readers from the New Testament book of Revelation).[2] The most significant departure may be the most subtle. Moroni's governing purpose in the book of Ether is to demonstrate the singular role of Jesus Christ as the source of all human salvation. Ether's revelation of a *second* sacred city wherein the faithful will be saved opens and expands Moroni's focus on singleness. Like sacramental wine poured and passed to a congregation, Christ's blood is in Ether's vision divided and distributed through geographic space.

Despite this difference in mood, the vision of Ether reaffirms key themes of the larger book in which it appears, an apt if unexpected conclusion to its theological message. Above all, Ether's vision underscores the central purpose for the inclusion of the Jaredite record with the Book of Mormon: namely, to show that Christ's saving grace excludes none, no matter how far flung in time or place or experience from the main body of Israel. We have seen how Moroni works to expand the circle of salvation, showing that faith is the means of salvation for the modern Gentiles who are an

☞ In its focus on the seed of Lehi, the vision of Ether echoes/prefigures the prophecy of Jesus Christ himself, who unfolds for the Nephites the raising of a new Jerusalem by the remnant of Jacob in 3 Nephi 21:23. It is surprising that Ether, a Jaredite prophet, would be familiar with the Abrahamic covenant, the sacred world of Israel, the lineage of the Lehi and Sariah, and Christ's future ministry among the Nephites. The text specifies that Ether "saw the days of Christ" (Ether 13:4), and he may have received prophetic foreknowledge of these events. Alternately, some scholars suggest that Moroni may have paraphrased Ether's vision using terms, images, and histories from the Nephite tradition, rather than from the underlying Jaredite text.[1]

ocean apart and millennia removed from the physical events of the atonement. He works out a new understanding of redemption in Christ in which ethnic identity plays no role, and Jews and Gentiles enjoy equal access based on faith and Spirit. His prophetic mind pushes further, dwelling on those who, like the brother of Jared before his theophany, have never heard the name of Christ and cannot call upon it. The vision of Ether underscores Moroni's expansive impulse. One meaning of Ether's vision of a second holy city, geographically separated from the first, is that there is a place for all, no matter how obscure or remote, in *local* gatherings of the saved. Amid the many mystical interpretations of New Jerusalem in Jewish and Christian scripture, the book of Ether offers a surprisingly concrete, earthbound vision of the new holy city to be raised at the end-times. It is, at least in part, a practical means of globally scaling up the availability of salvation in Christ. No soul is too far flung, it seems, for the prophetic minds of Moroni and Ether to seek her gathering to safety.

Moreover, the vision's emphasis on a chosen *land* as the center of God's providential work, rather than on a particular chosen people, underscores the book's critique of religious ethnocentrism. A key motif in the book of Ether is the wave-like rhythm of peoples sweeping on and off the shores of the choice land. Moroni's message is that the land belongs to God, not to any particular group. For early readers with ears to hear, this theme resonated against manifest destiny, the belief that US expansion across North America was inevitable and divinely justified. The book of Ether, by contrast, shows that inhabitants of the choice land are only tenants, subsisting by divine grace, not entitled claimants of an ethnic birthright. Moroni shows that the Jaredites and the Nephites were purged from the chosen land in twin tragedies of pride, violence, and unbelief. He warns modern Gentiles that the same catastrophe awaits them, if they reject this urgent call to repentance from ancient voices in the dust. Though Moroni considers the Gentiles' predicament at length, the book of Ether ends with a great question mark still remaining at its center: will the Gentiles receive the Book of Mormon with charity? Will they accept its invitation to repent and exercise faith in Christ? Or will they follow the path of the Jaredites and Nephites, and find themselves swept away from God's presence in the chosen land?

In contrast to the ambiguity surrounding the Gentiles, however, the future of the remnant of Joseph (understood by Moroni as the modern descendants of the Lamanites, the indigenous peoples of Book of Mormon lands) is prophesied boldly in the vision of Ether. Foreshadowed by the Lord's deliverance of the biblical Joseph and his father Israel in ancient times, the remnant of Joseph's seed in the chosen land will be saved in New Jerusalem, "and it shall be a land of their inheritance" (Ether 13:7–8). To this group alone, it seems, the chosen land is a *promised* land. But their claiming of that inheritance and their raising of the new city reverberate beyond Joseph's seed alone. The appearance of the New Jerusalem is a sign of the messianic renewal of the world, the prophesied time when all things pass away and "there shall be a new heaven and a new earth; and they shall be like unto the old save the old have passed away, and all things have become new" (verses 8–9).[3] It's a remarkable prophecy: the obscure indigenous remnant of an unknown branch of scattered Israel, brought low by nations briefly riding high on the carousel of history, will raise a holy city in a remote corner of the world, and this city will presage the cosmic events foretold by prophets and eagerly awaited by Jews and Christians the world over. A butterfly flaps its wings at the edge of the world, and a hurricane circles the heavens.

For Moroni and Ether, the specific historical and ethnic meanings of these events matter, because that specificity reveals in detail the shape of God's plan. But these specific historical events open onto a broader theological horizon. Moroni concludes his summary of Ether's great vision with the observation, "When these things come, bringeth to pass the scripture which saith, there are they who were first, who shall be last; and there are they who were last, who shall be first" (Ether 13:12). This is a brilliantly concise crystallization of the core themes and structural features of the book of Ether. It captures the restless cycle of peoples—Jaredites, Nephites, Gentiles—who arrive on the shores of the chosen land, thrive for a time in the warmth of God's bounty, rise high in pride, and are subsequently brought low. It captures the ethical message of Ether's great vision: the despised peoples of the land rise up first to greet the renewal of all things, by which every hidden and obscure thing will be known and blessed at last. It even captures the curious structural paradox of the book of Ether nested within the larger Book of Mormon, the "back to the future" quality by which the first *chronological* events narrated—the founding of the Jaredite people at the great tower and their subsequent history—appear (nearly) last in the textual order of the book.

Ether's vision is not the first appearance of a message of radical reversal in the Book of Mormon. Similar language describes Nephi$_1$'s great apocalyptic vision of God's work in the last days, wherein the revelations of the Jews and Gentiles are brought together and the sacred texts are transferred among peoples: "And after he has manifested himself unto the Jews and also unto the Gentiles, then he shall manifest himself unto the

Gentiles and also unto the Jews, and the last shall be first, and the first shall be last" (1 Ne. 13:42). And both passages echo Jesus's description of the reversal of worldly values in the kingdom of God: "And every one that hath forsaken houses, or brethren, or sisters, or father, or mother, or wife, or children, or lands, for my name's sake, shall receive an hundredfold, and shall inherit everlasting life. But many that are first shall be last; and the last shall be first" (Matt. 19:29–30).

Each of these passages points toward the profound renewal and revaluation that occurs at the reunion of Christ and his people in the kingdom of God. Theologians call this topic *eschatology*, while Church members tend to discuss it as the Second Coming. Neither term appears in the Book of Mormon. Indeed, the term *Second Coming* is especially out of place in the Book of Mormon, which shows that Jesus Christ has come to his people many times—to the Nephites and to the brother of Jared, at a minimum, as well as to the Book of Mormon prophets who testify that they have seen Christ. For Book of Mormon believers, *the Second Coming of Christ* is better understood simply as the "renewed presence of Christ," or the "renewal of all things."

Followers of Jesus Christ have long scrutinized their sacred texts for signs and portents that signal the coming renewal of all things. The figurative language of scripture complicates this effort of good-faith believers, making it difficult to interpret the text and the times and fomenting fear of apocalyptic destruction. I write this during the first spring of the 2020 coronavirus pandemic, as apocalyptic speculation flies between anxious believers. The structural logic of the book of Ether cuts through with simplifying clarity. Moroni deliberately constructs his redaction of the Jaredite record to draw a three-way parallel between the theophany of the brother of Jared, the visitation of Jesus Christ to the Nephites, and the renewed presence of Christ in the last days. Of the brother of Jared's mountaintop encounter, Moroni writes that "[Jesus Christ] ministered unto him even as he ministered unto the Nephites" (Ether 3:18); soon after, Moroni records the words of Christ to the peoples of the last days, writing that "when [they] shall rend that veil of unbelief"—a reference to the "veil" removed from the brother of Jared's eyes allowing him to see Christ—"I [will] manifest unto them the things which the brother of Jared saw" (Ether 4:15, 7). By aligning the three events structurally, Moroni emphasizes the core experience they share in common. Quite simply, as the Lord tells the brother of Jared, "ye are brought back into my presence" (Ether 3:13). Spare and simple, this core pattern is at the heart of individual and communal unions with Christ. It can occur at any time or place. It organizes key moments in the plan of salvation, from individual salvation, as the brother of Jared is "redeemed from the fall," to the founding of Zion communities, as occurs at the Nephite theophany, to the final renewal of Christ's presence in the end times. Like a skeleton key, the simple pattern of renewed presence with Christ unlocks the complex mysteries of sacred history. Christ comes—whether for the second, seventh, or thousandth time—every time believers abide with him.

To some it may seem anticlimactic to peer beneath the mysteries and great signs surrounding the Second Coming—and the book of Ether includes plenty of intriguing drama around the sealed portion of the brother of Jared's vision—only to find a simple, quiet core. Yet the vision of Ether, for all its vivid apocalyptic imagery, teaches that the renewal of all things does not occur by way of dramatic events and wild transformations: "And there shall be a new heaven and a new earth; and they shall be like unto the old save the old have passed away, and all things have become new" (Ether 13:9). Though all things will become new, they will be *like unto the old*, except that the old things have passed away. The renewed presence of Christ does not change the basic foundations of our experience—the limitation, the loss, the slow stepwise growth—but allows us to live and love in them better. We will better live and love the renewed but fundamentally unaltered conditions of our lives precisely because we will have learned that these things, too, pass away. Shakespeare knew it: "This thou perceiv'st, which makes thy love more strong, / To love that well which thou must leave ere long."[4] The vision of Ether shows us that all things become new in the vivifying grace of Christ, but they become new in the oldest way: by dying.

This insight draws together the central themes of the book of Ether. As we've come to expect from Moroni, a man whose longest and truest companions are the hissing voices of the Nephite scriptural archive, the renewal of all things is ultimately bound up with scripture. He thinks deeply—one might say obsessively—about the future of the book he writes. What kind of reception will it receive at the hands of modern readers? What kind of a world will it enter after its long interment? More importantly, how will it change the readers and the world it finds? He comes to understand that the Book of Mormon itself will catalyze the prophesied renewal of all things in the last days. At the coming forth of the book, the voice of Christ explains, "my revelations which I have caused to be written by my servant John [shall] be unfolded in the eyes of all the people. Remember, when ye see these things, ye shall know that the time is at hand that they shall be made manifest in very deed. Therefore, when ye shall receive this record ye may know that the work of the Father has commenced" (Ether 4:16–17). The coming forth of "*these* things" sets in motion the renewal of *all* things. The appearance of the Book of Mormon ushers in the renewed presence of Christ.

From one perspective, it might seem that Moroni was simply wrong on several counts. The Book of Mormon appeared in print in March 1830. If we take that historical occurrence to mark the "coming forth" of the book, and if we take its reception among early American readers to be the measure of its meaning, we would rightly conclude that the Gentiles as a whole rejected the book and that it failed in its mission. And if we understand the Second Coming as a dramatic and singular alteration of history, we would likewise conclude that the Book of Mormon failed to catalyze its transformation.

But the book of Ether teaches us to see the coming forth of scripture as a constellation of microevents, a tiny point of light each time a reader opens the book and receives its word with charity. And it teaches us to see the renewal of all things in the ordinary passing away of our worlds from day to day. When we open its pages with the intent to receive, the Book of Mormon unfolds as scripture in our eyes. The work of the Father commences. A veil drops. We are brought back into God's presence.

Further Reading

Hardy, Grant. *Understanding the Book of Mormon: A Reader's Guide* (New York: Oxford University Press, 2010).

Hickman, Jared. "The Book of Mormon as Amerindian Apocalypse," *American Literature 86*, no. 3 (Durham, NC: Duke University Press, 2014), 429–61.

Holland, David F. *Sacred Borders: Continuing Revelation and Canonical Restraint in Early America* (New York: Oxford University Press, 2011).

Miller, Adam S. "A Hermeneutics of Weakness," in *Rube Goldberg Machines: Essays in Mormon Theology* (Sandy, UT: Greg Kofford Books, 2012), 99–105.

Spencer, Joseph M. *An Other Testament: On Typology* (Salem, OR: Salt Press, 2016).

——. "Christ and Krishna: The Vision of Arjuna and the Brother of Jared," *Journal of Book of Mormon Studies* 23, no. 1 (Provo, UT: Neal A. Maxwell Institute for Religious Scholarship, 2014), 56–80.

Thomas, Catherine M. "The Brother of Jared at the Veil," in *Temples of the Ancient World: Ritual and Symbolism* (Salt Lake City, UT: Deseret Book, 1994), 388–398.

Welch, John W. "Preliminary Comments on the Sources behind the Book of Ether," in *FARMS Preliminary Report*, (Provo, UT: Foundation for Ancient Research and Mormon Studies (FARMS 1986)).

Williams, Rowan. *Christ the Heart of Creation* (London: Bloomsbury Continuum, 2018).

Endnotes

SERIES INTRODUCTION

1. Elder Neal A. Maxwell, "The Children of Christ," university devotional, Brigham Young University, Provo, UT, 4 February 1990, https://speeches.byu.edu/talks/neal–a–maxwell_children–christ/.

2. Elder Neal A. Maxwell, "The Inexhaustible Gospel," university devotional, Brigham Young University, Provo, UT, 18 August 1992, https://speeches.byu.edu/talks/neal–a–maxwell/ inexhaustible–gospel/.

3. Elder Neal A. Maxwell, "The Book of Mormon: A Great Answer to 'The Great Question,'" address, Book of Mormon Symposium, Brigham Young University, Provo, UT, 10 October 1986, reprinted in *The Voice of My Servants: Apostolic Messages on Teaching, Learning, and Scripture,* ed. Scott C. Esplin and Richard Neitzel Holzapfel (Provo, UT: Religious Studies Center, Brigham Young University; Salt Lake City: Deseret Book, 2010), 221–38, https://rsc.byu.edu/archived/ voice-my–servants/book–mormon–great–answer–great–question.

INTRODUCTION

1. It is unclear why Mormon includes nothing about the matter in his account of Christ's ministry.

2. My summary is indebted to the structural analysis of Grant Hardy in *Understanding the Book of Mormon* (see p. 236), and to his editorial subheadings in the Maxwell Institute Study Edition of the Book of Mormon. Grant Hardy, *The Book of Mormon: Another Testament of Jesus Christ, Maxwell Institute Study Edition*, ed. Grant Hardy (Provo, UT: Neal A. Maxwell Institute for Religious Scholarship, 2018).

3. Francine R. Bennion, "A Latter-day Saint Theology of Suffering," in *At the Pulpit: 185 Years of Discourses by Latter-day Saint Women*, ed. Jennifer Reeder and Kate Holbrook (Salt Lake City, UT: The Church Historian's Press, 2017), 217.

1

1. Grant Hardy, *Understanding the Book of Mormon: A Reader's Guide* (New York: Oxford University Press, 2010), 235–40.

2. See, for instance, John W. Welch, "Preliminary Comments on the Sources behind the Book of Ether," in *F.A.R.M.S. Preliminary Report, 1986* (Provo, UT: Foundation for Ancient Research and Mormon Studies); and Brant Gardner, *Second Witness: Analytical and Contextual Commentary on the Book of Mormon, vol. 6, Fourth Nephi through Moroni* (Salt Lake City, UT: Greg Kofford Books, 2011).

3. See, for instance, 1 Nephi 15:12–20 and Mormon 5:10–24.

4. Joseph Spencer, "Christ and Krishna: The Vision of Arjuna and the Brother of Jared," *Journal of Book of Mormon Studies* 23, no. 1 (Provo, UT: Neal A. Maxwell Institute for Religious Scholarship, 2014), 72.

5. Jeffrey R. Holland, "Rending the Veil of Unbelief," in *The Voice of My Servants: Apostolic Messages on Teaching, Learning, and Scripture*, ed. Scott C. Esplin and Richard Neitzel Holzapfel (Provo, UT: Religious Studies Center, Brigham Young University; Salt Lake City, UT: Deseret Book, 2010), 143–64, https://rsc.byu.edu/voice-my-servants/rending-veil-unbelief.

6. In chapter 4, I argue that the sixteen stones are figuratively coded by Moroni as a divine text.

7. Joseph M. Spencer, Adam S. Miller, *An Other Testament: On Typology* (Salem, OR: Salt Press, 2016); Adam Miller, *An Early Resurrection: Life in Christ before You Die* (Salt Lake City, UT: Deseret Book, 2018).

8. In chapter 4, I address Moroni's intense authorial anxiety.

2

1. I draw heavily here on chapter 3 of Joseph Spencer's *An Other Testament: On Typology*. See Joseph M. Spencer, *An Other Testament: On Typology* (Salem, OR: Salt Press, 2016), 69–104.

2. See, for instance, Mosiah 15:11; Alma 13:2; Alma 25:15; and Helaman 8:22, among many.

3. See, for instance, Mormon's summary of the Anti-Nephi-Lehies' understanding of the gospel and law at Alma 25:15–16.

4. Joseph Spencer offers a definitive exploration of the temporality of Alma 36 in chapter 1 of *An Other Testament.* See Joseph M. Spencer, *An Other Testament: On Typology* (Salem, OR: Salt Press, 2016), 1–32.

3

1. Grant Hardy pioneered the narratorial study of the Book of Mormon with his landmark work *Understanding the Book of Mormon,* and my analysis of Moroni as an active narrative agency owes much to his approach. Hardy addresses Moroni's narrative strategies in his chapters 8 and 9. See Grant Hardy, *Understanding the Book of Mormon: A Reader's Guide* (New York: Oxford University Press, 2010), 217–267.

2. Here I summarize the sweeping prophecies of 1 Nephi 12–13 and 2 Nephi 26–29.

3. Ezra Taft Benson, *The Teachings of Ezra Taft Benson* (Salt Lake City, UT: Bookcraft, 1988), 569.

4. Part of the reason for this lacuna is certainly the restriction of the brother of Jared's vision until after the time of Christ's coming (see Ether 3:21).

5. See Hardy, *Understanding the Book of Mormon*, 235.

4

1. See also Mormon 3:20; 5:8–9, 12; 8:16, 25, 33–34; 9:35–36; Ether 3:17, 24–27; 4:8, 11, 16; 5:3–6; 8:26; 12:22–23; Moroni 10:3–4, 26–28.

2. *American Dictionary of the English Language*, s.v. "thing," http://webstersdictionary1828.com/Dictionary/thing.

3. Intriguingly, it is the Book of Mormon's first and last writers who are most aware of the book's future readers' response: the theme appears often in 1 and 2 Nephi, and in 3 Nephi, Mormon, Ether, and Moroni. See, for instance: 1 Nephi 13:35; 2 Nephi 27:6; 30:3; 3 Nephi 21:2; Mormon 5:12–14, 8:34; Ether 4:6, 8; 12:22–29; Moroni 10:27.

4. See David F. Holland, *Sacred Borders: Continuing Revelation and Canonical Restraint in Early America* (New York: Oxford University Press, 2011).

5. See Grant Hardy, "The Book of Mormon as Post-Canonical Scripture," in *The Expanded Canon: Perspectives on Mormonism and Sacred Texts* (Salt Lake City, UT: Greg Kofford Books, 2018).

6. Grant Hardy, *Understanding the Book of Mormon: A Reader's Guide* (New York: Oxford University Press, 2010), 224.

7. Jeffrey R. Holland, "Rending the Veil of Unbelief," in *The Voice of My Servants: Apostolic Messages on Teaching, Learning, and Scripture*, ed. Scott C. Esplin and Richard Neitzel Holzapfel (Provo, UT: Religious Studies Center, Brigham Young University; Salt Lake City, UT: Deseret Book, 2010), 143–64. https://rsc.byu.edu/archived/voice-my-servants/rending-veil-unbelief

8. Holland, "Rending the Veil," 152.

9. See Rowan Williams, *Christ the Heart of Creation* (London: Bloomsbury Continuum, 2018); John Caputo, *The Weakness of God: A Theology of the Event* (Bloomington: Indiana University Press, 2006).

CONCLUSION

1. See John W. Welch, "Preliminary Comments on the Sources behind the Book of Ether" (FARMS Preliminary Report, 1986), 8–9; and Brant Gardner, *Second Witness*, vol. 6, *4th Nephi–Moroni,* (Salt Lake City, UT: Greg Kofford Books, 2007), 303–306.

2. See 1 Nephi 12:10; Alma 5:21; 13:11; 34:36; 3 Nephi 27:19; Revelation 7:9–17. On the New Jerusalem, see Revelation 21:1–5.

3. See Jared Hickman, "The Book of Mormon as Amerindian Apocalypse," *American Literature* 86, no. 3 (Durham, NC: Duke University Press, 2014), 429–61.

4. Shakespeare, William, "Sonnet 73: That Time of Year Thou Mayst in Me Behold," Poetry Foundation, www.poetryfoundation.org/poems/45099/sonnet-73-that-time-of-year-thou-mayst-in-me-behold.

Index

110

111

Colophon

The text of the book is typeset in Arnhem,
Fred Smeijer's 21st-century-take on late
18th-century Enlightenment-era letterforms
known for their sturdy legibility and clarity
of form. Captions and figures are typset in
Quaadraat Sans, also by Fred Smeijers.
The book title and chapter titles are typeset
in Thema by Nikola Djurek.

Printed on Domtar Lynx 74 gsm,
Forest Stewardship Council (FSC) Certified.

Printed by Brigham Young University Print & Mail Services

Woodcut illuminations **Brian Kershisnik**
Illumination consultation **Faith Heard**

Book design & typography **Douglas Thomas**
Production typesetting **Maria Camargo**

Ether 3:6 ... the Lord stretched forth his hand and touched the stones one by one with his finger.